THE PLACE OF CONFLUENT EDUCATION IN THE HUMAN POTENTIAL MOVEMENT

A Historical Perspective

Stewart B. Shapiro

University Press of America,® Inc.
Lanham • New York • Oxford

Library of Congress Cataloging-in-Publication Data

Shapiro, Stewart Bennett.
The place of confluent education in the human potential movement :
a historical perspective / Stewart B. Shapiro.
p.   cm.
Includes bibliographical references and index.
1. Education, Humanistic. 2. Gestalt psychology. I. Title
LC1011.S44 1998   370.11'2—dc21   98-24302   CIP

ISBN 0-7618-1186-9 (cloth: alk. ppr.)

⊖™ The paper used in this publication meet the minimum
requirements of American National Standard for information
Sciences—Permanence of Paper for Printed Library Materials,
ANSI Z39.48—1984

Dedication

This Book is Dedicated to my Wife, Lover, Colleague, and Friend, Muriel T. Shapiro for her constant encouragement, constructive feedback and many hours of reflective discussion of this work and related topics.

Contents

Figures

Tables

List of Abbreviations

ACE	Association of Confluent Educators
AERA	American Educational Research Association
ASCD	American Society of Curriculum and Development
ANOVA	Analysis of Variance
CE	Confluent Education
CE	Concrete Experience = Learning Mode on the Learning Styles Inventory
CEDARC	Confluent Education Development and Research Center
CPAP	Committee on Academic Personnel
DRICE	Development and Research in Confluent Education
ELO	Educational Leadership and Organizations
ENFJ	Extroverted Intuitive Feeling Type on the MBTI and K
EPOL	Educational Policy, Organizations and Leadership (Program at UCSB)
F	Feeling Function on the MBTI and K
GSE	Graduate School of Education (UCSB)
HCIACS	Humanistic/Confluent Interactional Analysis Category System
HRD	Human Resources Development
HTHL	Human Teaching for Human Learning (G. I. Brown)
J	Judgment Function on the MBTI and K
K	The Kiersey Temperament Sorter
K-6	Kindergarten Through Sixth Grade in Schools

K-12	Kindergarten Through Twelfth Grade in Schools
LIT	Literature
LSD	Lysergic Acid Diethylamide
LSI	Learning Styles Inventory
MA	Master of Arts
MBTI	The Myers-Briggs Type Indicator
MD	Doctor of Medicine
MDiv	Master of Divinity
MFCC	Marriage, Family and Child Counseling (License)
MSW	Master of Social Work
N	Number (of cases)
N	Intuitive Function on the MBTI and K
NDD	Neurosis, Disease and Discontent
"NFs"	Intuitive-Feeling Type on the MBTI and K
NTL	National Training Laboratories
OTL	Orientation to Learning (Scales)
OTL $B_1 B_2$	Alternate Form of OTL
P	Perception Function on the MBTI and K
PhD	Doctor of Philosophy
RN	Registered Nurse
SIG	Special Interest Group (In American Educational Research Association)
TOTL	Transpersonal Orientation to Learning (Scales)
UC	University of California
UCLA	University of California, Los Angeles
UCSB	University of California, Santa Barbara
USA	United States of America
WASC	Western Association of Schools and Colleges
WASP	White, Anglo-Saxon Protestant
"Y"	A Management Theory (D. McGregor)

Foreword

In *The Place of Confluent Education in the Human Potential Movement: A Historical Perspective*, Stewart Shapiro takes us on a comprehensive journey through Confluent Education. He helps us understand that apparently the roots of Confluent Education go back over 20 centuries to the "self-actualizing" philosophy of Aristotle. He also tells us that we are part of a deep, recurrent "Humanist Impulse."

I never cease to be amazed by Shapiro's insight. For example, his data show that while the Confluent faculty recruited a cohort with remarkably similar values, they came from widely disparate backgrounds. The common element was disillusionment with traditional education.

Yes, many of us sought refuge in the Confluent program. We saw it as having an almost magical potential for liberating us from the unnecessary constraints of conventional academia. The promise of the program was fulfilled in myself and many others.

However, we discovered that implementing our innovative, humanistic approach in the "real world" was met with formidable resistance by those who were also unaware of their own subjectivity. Many of these well-intentioned practitioners felt that their own personal feelings and expressions of affect by their students/clients were not appropriate for curricula or consultation.

Shapiro asserts that Confluent Education, like all other interventions, is context-embedded. Generally, without a supportive context, we can expect little institutional access or change.

In his last substantive chapter, Stewart Shapiro points to three kinds of legacies from Confluent Education. These are the institutional, the professional, and the cultural. These legacies serve to remind us that although the program, per se, has been terminated, some of the effects of Confluent Education are still significantly active.

Like Sisyphus, perhaps, we have discovered that all change, personal, professional, and social, is fraught with conflict, resistance, and challenge. However, if we realize that we are part of a much larger Human Potential Movement, which arises out of reactions to our discontent, it might help us to see our place in history and enable us to continue on our mission.

Phillip Moheno, Ph.D.   November 10, 1997
San Diego Research
La Jolla, California

Preface

As UC professor Ruth Rosen (1997) has remarked in *The Los Angeles Times*, "Our culture encourages historical amnesia." It appears to me that the subculture of Confluent Education also followed that pattern. Unfortunately, much of the "here and now" bias of the working chair in Gestalt was mindlessly transferred to the ideology of the Confluent Program. We never self-studied our origins, such as Third Force Psychology, Existentialism, Phenomenology, Humanism, etc. (see Chapter 2). Fortunately, this was not necessarily the case in the institutional legacy of Confluent Education (see Chapter 4).

The time is now ripe for presenting some perspectives on Confluent Education, a 27-year program at the University of California, Santa Barbara, because this historic program is past its final transition—its terminal stage. Tracing some of the major patterns/fortunes of this program from its inception to now might provide us with insights into its history and meaning and into the survival/demise of innovative movements within the larger context of a traditional, research-based university, like UCSB.

Confluent Education is a major variant in the Humanistic Education genre, "with a strong Gestalt backbone" (Simpson, 1976), although the most recent applications have been *beyond* therapy, *beyond* personal growth, and also primarily *beyond* the K-12 classroom. The recent applications have been mostly to organizations and executives, many outside of educational institutions.

On a more personal note, as my good friend, Brian Burke, pointed out, this book is also a product of my own continuing search for identity. The book helps me to define the *place* of *Confluent Education* in terms of a much larger movement. It provides a context for interpreting that place. While Humanistic Psychology is my primary professional identification, I spent 27 fruitful years applying it to

Confluent Education in the latter half of my professional career.

I think this book fairly represents my basic ambivalence toward Confluent Education along with Humanistic Education, Humanistic Psychology, and the whole Human Potential Movement. While the "scientist" in me in many respects is critical, the "humanist" part of me respects and admires nearly all these programs/movements—personally and professionally.

In closing, I feel I should accept responsibility for my part in whatever shortcomings or contributions Confluent Education has had to offer. Apparently, I and many others were so caught up in the exciting, innovative, and partially rebellious nature of this controversial program that we did not or could not see the need for significant adaptation before it was "too late." Nevertheless, whatever Confluent Education was and is, I regard it as a significant expression of the Human Potential Movement and that historic "Humanist Impulse" which has been recurring for millennia.

Acknowledgments

I recognize and deeply appreciate the contributions which others have made to this project. In addition to Muriel, my wife, the three most helpful resources were Thomas Greening, David Russell, and Phillip Moheno. They were especially valuable in the first chapter and in the idea of expanding an article in the *Journal of Humanistic Psychology* on the history of the UCSB Confluent Education Program to this complete book. I am also grateful for the editorial input and encouragement I received from the editorial board of the Journal of Humanistic Psychology.

Vicki Stevenson, my editorial assistant, has been indispensable with her friendly competence and editorial knowledge.

In the field interviews, I appreciated the leaders and staff of the four institutions which exemplify the ongoing legacy of Confluent Education. These people include Kent Ferguson, Brian Burke, Jill Wallerstedt, Steve O. Lane, Georgia Kimminger, of the Santa Barbara Middle School; Stephen Aizenstat, founder of the Pacifica Graduate Institute; Thomas Yoemans, founder of the Concord Institute; and Liv Grendstat and Mark Rousseau of the Meta-senter in Norway.

My UCSB colleagues, Larry Beutler and Naftaly Glasman; Dennis Naiman, recently retired from the Goleta Union School District; and Ann Lippincott of the UCSB Teacher Education Program provided important counsel and referral agents for field interviews.

In the Goleta Schools, I interviewed four administrators/teachers whose work epitomized for me the professional legacy of Confluent Education in the local public schools. They are Lisa Maglione, Susan Whisenand, Susan Perona, and Robert Wood.

I'm certain there were others from whom I received interest in and encouragement for writing this book—(they all promised to buy a copy!).

To all of the above, my deep appreciation—a book, after all, is a social project, and without their support, it would have been extremely difficult, if possible at all.

Introduction

This book is an expansion of a recently published article. It appeared in the *Journal of Humanistic Psychology*, summer 1997. I received so much support for my study of "The UCSB Confluent Education Program: Its Essence and Demise," that I decided to fill out my account of this historic program by adding reflections on its origins, a critique and its legacy.

The major premise of the book is that Confluent Education was and is embedded in the broad Human Potential Movement, which was embodied by the Esalen Institute in the early 1960s, and lasted until the early 1980s. This movement, in turn, I think is also embedded in a much larger movement, often referred to as an awakening, a revolution in consciousness or a new philosophy. Thus, the title of this book reminds us of the original place of Confluent Education at a time of cultural instability, when political, social, scientific, and cultural paradigms were shifting rapidly. I also think of this in the context of a recurring humanizing force—a release of pent up human-centered strivings and yearnings which break free to expression—and, unfortunately, often to excess and backlash.

In my view, what I call the "Humanist Impulse" has erupted sporadically, historically beginning with the ancient Greeks and continuing throughout the modern period.

Examples of this erupting Humanist Impulse are the ancient Greek civilization; the Renaissance; the French and Scottish Enlightenments; the Transcendental movement of Rousseau, Emerson, Whitman; and many others in science, politics, literature, art, music, and history.

I regard the Human Potential Movement itself as a manifestation of the modern period's eruption of this "Humanist Impulse" in history. Others (e.g., Lamont, 1982, pp. 19, 60) have referred to the "Humanist Spirit" and I regard that as synonymous with the Humanist Impulse.

I have chosen this book as an instrument to address the culture-wide "historical amnesia" to which Rosen has referred. Unfortunately, many of us in Confluent Education, with our affective and "here-and-now" biases, have also demonstrated this neglect of our roots.

In the first chapter, originally the article, I present some of the highlights of our program's history; political forces; some original, empirical, longitudinal data on the students of this program; a summary for an empirical perspective, including personality and learning styles; and a cultural/contextual interpretation of what happened to this program. In the second chapter, I provide detailed accounts of the origins of this program in the context of the Human Potential Movement. The third chapter is intended as a coherent and much needed critique and, in the fourth chapter, I detail what I believe to be the legacy of Confluent Education. The summary and interpretation emphasize what I see as the most significant features of Confluent Education, its embeddedness in the Human Potential Movement as a manifestation of the historic Humanist Impulse and, finally, its contributions to the lessons to be learned from its rich and varied history.

What made Confluent Education different from other academic programs was its emphasis on the nurturance and development of individual and unique human beings, personally and professionally. Throughout the years of this program, the most lasting values were actualized in the context of a *personalized* learning community. Most academic programs have a conceptual agenda, including theory and research, often *at the cost of* personal knowledge and a sense of community.

Chapter 1

The UCSB Confluent Education Program: Its Essence and Demise[1]

Historical Perspective

The program known as Confluent Education emerged at UCSB in 1966 through the work of professor George I. Brown and is documented in the book he edited, *Human Teaching for Human Learning* (1971), supported by a 3-year Ford-Esalen grant (1966-70).

George Brown was the "father-figure" of this program. He had the vision to pull together and apply to education some of the exciting ideas and experiences that were occurring in North America and Europe in the mid and late 1960s known as *The Human Potential Movement*. I met George through my work on exploring "positive experience" at Esalen Institute at Big Sur, California. Both of us saw a deep experiential and theoretical connection between our respective approaches to personal growth. As I understand it, the Confluent Education Program grew out of George's "Creativity Project," which was a research and development program in the Goleta and Santa Barbara schools.

From the "Creativity Project" and George's contact with Fritz Perls, whom he met at Esalen (around 1965), George apparently had a "conversion-reaction" to Gestalt practices. Through his contact with Perls and Gestalt came the idea of "confluence" which originally was regarded as a dysfunctional union of individual identity with others or with traditional cultural norms. Confluence was analogous to some of the more primitive psychoanalytic ego defenses against existential

[1]Chapter 1 is an adapted version from my article with the same title in *The Journal of Humanistic Psychology* (1997, Summer), *37*(3), 79-104. Reprinted by permission of Sage Publications.

anxiety and the difficulties of full individuality.

Brown, however, with the help of his public school teacher-colleagues (especially Gloria Castillo, Aaron Hillman, and Robin Montz, local teachers of elementary school and secondary literature and social studies) reframed and broadened the concept of confluence to apply to the integration of affect and cognition in teaching and learning. Through the years, George and his colleagues extended and broadened the original "confluence" and Gestalt principles to organizations and systems theory (Merry & Brown, 1987), and these principles ultimately became the major application of this program.

Shortly after the Confluent Education Program was initiated and officially accepted in the Education Department at UCSB in 1968, the Ph.D. degree program became established in 1970. Around the time I joined (full-time), it became a full program at UCSB, initially staffed by two senior, tenured professors. There were 10-15 M.A. students and soon after that, 3-4 Ph.D. candidates.

My own background influenced my role in Confluent Education. This includes the private practice of clinical and organizational psychology for 17 years, beginning in 1950, when I received my Ph.D. in Clinical Psychology at the University of Southern California. After that length of time in professional practice, I felt burned out and intellectually unfulfilled. I came to UCSB in the fall of 1967 as the Director of the newly formed Counseling and Guidance Program in the Department of Education. After a few years as Director of that program, I realized that I did not fit well in an administrative role.

From the time I came to UCSB and joined the Confluent Program, George and his group of nine local teachers were at work at Esalen, developing the Ford-Esalen Project out of which came the first book on Confluent Education. That book, *Human Teaching for Human Learning*, is original source material for a history of this program.

In 1971 we began to attract students from all over this country and the world. One of the noteworthy features of this program is that the backgrounds of the students have been quite heterogeneous: disciplines, gender, nationality, ethnicity, ages, etc. However, when these diverse people came together they appeared to have very similar social and educational values. In my quantitative studies I have painstakingly measured what these broadly held concerns were, primarily in terms of instructional or applied values (Shapiro, 1985a, 1985b, 1987). There was wide general agreement on application of these principles to instruction, counseling, and clinical/organizational consulting.

We continued in the original mode of emphasizing Gestalt, group dynamics, and other experiential approaches in the classroom until Mark Phillips joined us in 1973. He was one of the first Ph.D.s to graduate from the then new Humanistic Education Program at the University of Massachusetts. One of the very few complete academic programs of this kind, it focused on the role of affect in learning, values clarification, and student empowerment. Mark Phillips had 10 years experience as a high school social studies teacher in Long Island, New York, and when he joined us we then had three full time professors. That was the "high water-mark" in our history.

Our failure to grow further was a very significant sign of the limits of academic acceptance of our unorthodox program in the Education Department at UCSB. This was very frustrating to both the faculty and students because several times we applied for more positions based on the number of students we had and the recognition we were getting outside of academia, in the public schools, in personal growth institutes like Esalen, and in agencies like the Ford Foundation.

Since 1979 we had been "limping along" with 2 2/3 positions. But we still *appeared* to be a thriving program in terms of the number and maturity of the students, especially those completing the Ph.D. program. However, they were perceived by the faculty to be very unevenly distributed in terms of academic respectability, and the research output of the Confluent faculty was not highly regarded in quality and quantity (1975-1980).

Shortly after Mark Phillips' arrival (1973), George Brown received a Ford Foundation grant for $350,000 over a 4-year period, known as Development and Research in Confluent Education "DRICE" (1970-74) (Simpson, 1976). It included many schools and up to 40-50 collaborators, mostly teachers, administrators, and consultants. The output primarily consisted of Confluent-types of curricula, applied to a very wide spectrum of educational institutions, from early childhood to the university level, and professional schools.

Out of DRICE came the 1975 book, *The Live Classroom*, edited by George Brown. Like the Ford-Esalen work, DRICE was almost entirely applied to classroom teachers, teaching methods, and new ways of reaching students. It emphasized both the personal and professional development of teachers.

Next came the "Ford-Chicano" grant, about 1978, which included six

Latino Ph.D. candidates in Confluent Education, four of whom eventually earned their Ph.D.s. This remains the deepest crosscultural endeavor in the history of the Confluent Education, excluding the extensive work in Norway.

In 1979-1980, Mark Phillips, not having received tenure a few years earlier, left UCSB to become the head of Secondary Education at San Francisco State University and Laurence Iannaccone joined the Confluent Program. Two thirds of his position was applied to Confluent Education and one third was attached to the program in Educational Administration.

With the coming of Larry Iannaccone there was a major shift in the scope and emphasis of the program toward political and organization issues, partly because of Larry's influence in the field of the politics of education and partly because George Brown's center of interest also changed from classroom applications to organizational issues both within and outside of education.

The program could be perceived as having three areas of strength but arranged somewhat differently than before. There was still a strong personal growth component via George and his wife, Judith Brown, a clear interpersonal and small group focus from myself, and a new third track at the organizational and political level, including socialization and viewing organizations as "learning systems," which came largely from Larry Iannaccone. Over time more and more of our applications were to organizations and leadership outside of the public schools. This was a very important transition, especially at the Ph.D. level, with increasing emphasis on research in the areas mentioned above.

The next big change came when I retired in 1991, followed by the retirement of George Brown in 1992. These retirements were "marker-events" in the program and signaled its coming demise a few years later (in 1993). The two faculty positions were never filled. Courses were taught on a temporary basis by instructors. We had fewer than one professorial faculty member when we were in the midst of recruiting replacements for Brown and Shapiro, but we had three "unsuccessful" searches and conducted a fourth unsuccessful search. In addition, Larry Iannaccone announced his retirement at the end of the 1993-94 academic year.

As of winter 1995, the Confluent and Educational Policy, Organizations and Leadership programs have been merged into a new program, Educational Leadership and Organizations (ELO), but the most recent search for a replacement did not include a Confluent component.

With the fall quarter of 1993 there was no longer an identifiable program in Confluent Education. No new M.A. or Ph.D. students were admitted to this formerly separate program, even through *technically* the program is still "on the books," because of the people still finishing their M.A.s and Ph.D.s in Confluent Education.

Political Perspective

From its beginning, Confluent Education has remained controversial, although active resistance and outright opposition to it has waxed and waned. At times there were various degrees of understanding and acceptance among our academic reference groups. A few people in the Education Department at UCSB openly supported us, when, for instance, our contributions to teacher education became recognized. However, over most of the life span of the program, the majority of professors and administrators were ambivalent, uninformed, and disinterested. Some were overtly negative because of perceived academic weakness due to the lack of rigorous quantitative research-oriented publications and unorthodox subjective, "touchy-feely" teaching methods and a lack of a sound, testable knowledge base.

The UCSB faculty and administrators across campus usually varied from very critical to ambivalent about us. One of our M.A. students (Brown, 1985) completed his Master's Project on the attitudes towards us of administrators and faculty across campus and within the Graduate School of Education. He found that most people "didn't know what in the hell Confluent Education was or did, but they were against it!" And this perception was confirmed by several off-campus reviewing committees. One of these groups could see "no empirical basis for the existence of Confluent Education as a separate, identifiable program" in the Department of Education.

Our program was regarded as a kind of "flaky, touchy-feely" holdover from the counter-culture of the 1960s, and to some extent this is understandable. And a considerable number of people in the local public schools and in the community were very negative about us. A right-wing group had us on a "Satan list." We were considered by them as essentially evil and certainly subversive to mainstream American family values and religion.

From other university sources there was some pallid support in the name of academic freedom and creativity, but as I have come to reflect on this situation, my impression is that even a considerable number of our own graduates were at least ambivalent about us, or did not want to be professionally identified with us. Like our academic peers, they were struggling for recognition from a powerful academic and professional elite.

Early in our history (circa 1967-73), we did have considerable external support due to the innovative nature of our approach in schools. We were part of that wave of human potential and humanistic optimism which swept the country in many institutions in the community and in many regions of the USA. This was true also in the public schools and not limited to California.

It is noteworthy that we had strong, direct political support in the State Legislature from John Vasconcellos, who was, for many years, Chairman of the powerful Ways and Means Committee in the State Assembly. I think that John's and a few of his colleagues' direct political power may have saved our program during earlier crises.

As events developed, much of what was innovative in the Confluent sense (e.g., Gestalt in the classroom, human interaction groups in industry) has now become part of the mainstream in some public school settings. Humanistic practices under labels different from "Confluent" or "Humanistic" have appeared and have been maintained, as in Cooperative Learning and the Self-Esteem movements.

The three Ford Foundation grants also legitimized and implemented our cause. They reflected the priorities of those times and provided clear evidence of support. But despite those grants, and direct, overt support from John Vasconcellos, the program which received them has never rested easily within the Education Department, the Graduate School of Education, and the general academic power structure at UCSB. The latter was represented, for example, by the Graduate Council, the Committee on Academic Personnel (CPAP), and the office of the Vice-Chancellor for Academic Affairs.

In summing up this part of this chapter, I offer some descriptions and sociopolitical impressions of our program.

I see Confluent Education at UCSB (and perhaps elsewhere) as a "haven for counter-culture refugees." Many, if not most of our students, came from academic or professional fields with which they were dissatisfied. Some were deeply disillusioned with traditional education, traditional organizational consulting, traditional counseling/psychotherapy, and traditional administration/management. Some were "refugees" from law, medicine, architecture, the ministry, etc., and from the arts of writing, acting, painting, dance, etc. My central confluent metaphor, however, is that of a heart of an alien humanoid transplanted into an American whose own "heart" has failed. Not only are we "alien tissue," we are "alien tissue" from an alien group.

Three kinds of questions occur to me before turning to a third major perspective on Confluent Education:

1.   What is and has been the central contribution of Confluent Education? Is that contribution well understood, well researched, well documented, and well implemented in schools and other institutions in our society and other societies? Is this contribution summarized and integrated in one source where people and scholars can readily refer to it?

2.   Why have we been so controversial—both within and outside of the academy?

3.   Under what conditions can Confluent Education continue to exist and contribute? Will there be *new forms* of Confluent Education in the current amalgamation of this program with the Educational Leadership and Organizations program?

My response to the first line of questions is "no," generally speaking. In all the significant and plentiful work, all the publications, books, articles, grants, seminars, presentations, Ph.D. dissertations and Master's Degree projects in these 27 years of study and application we still can't readily define it nor interpret the theory and outcomes very well. Phenomenology, Constructivism, Social Systems theory, and Sociolinguistic theory have been mentioned as theoretical successors to Gestalt theory, but there is no general consensus on these paradigms as far as I know. For our life span of 27 years (1966-1993), we were unable to delineate three or four major principles which comprised a clear conceptual nexus and made a difference in theory and practice.

From conversations with many people involved with this approach and from my own observations and studies, we seem to *feel* the significant differences Confluent Education can make in many situations, but a substantial conceptual case for these cannot be readily made. Most of us still appear to have difficulty in documenting, let alone explaining to educators, academics, and the community what

Confluent Education is and does.

With regard to the second question of the controversial status of Confluent Education, I will offer my cultural interpretation later in this chapter.

Responses to the third set of questions involving the current status of Confluent approaches in Educational Leadership and Organizations, only time will tell. Conditions in the Graduate School of Education are changing rapidly at the time of this writing due to the general cutbacks in the whole UC system, as well as the new Educational Leadership and Organizations merger and continuing difficulties in the search to replace the retired and retiring faculty from Confluent Education. However, in my opinion, Teacher Education has been significantly changed by the continued input of several Confluent instructors and supervisors.

Summary of Prior Empirical Data

In addition to the perspectives of the history and politics of Confluent Education, and its controversial status, what follows is a summary for an empirical, research-based perspective, based on previously published data.

In response to our conceptual identity problem:

1. A description of the Humanistic Education experts' and students' predominant instructional values has been generated (Shapiro, 1984, 1985a, 1985b, 1986, 1987).

2. A content analysis of samples of the writings from 40 and later expanded to 89 experts in Humanistic Education was submitted to multivariate analysis. These analyses were both for unrotated "principal components" and for rotated factor loadings. It is important to underline, however, that less than 5% of the original pool of OTL items were derived directly from experts in Confluent Education. So the OTL reflects a broad spectrum (100 "pieces" from 89 authors) of *Humanistic but not specifically Confluent Educators.*

Both analyses revealed five major factors, that varied in details of composition and relative strength, which is to be expected in these kinds of statistical techniques. Despite some variation, these analyses represent ways of getting to the underlying themes of humanistic instruction and therefore, by inference, to Confluent themes, which *could suggest a paradigm for Confluent Education.* This is not a very difficult inference for me to make because of the very high endorsement of the OTL instructional values by Confluent students (see page 13). The Confluent group mean OTL score for 8 years was *above* the 75th percentile of graduate students in Education at UCSB.

The above analyses can be viewed as a bridge from specific data to a conceptual interpretation (paradigm) of what these data mean, taken together.[2]

I chose to focus primarily on the "rotated" multivariate analysis, which represents a method of spreading the variance somewhat evenly among the viable factors found. I found the following five factors in the rotated multivariate analysis:

I.   The General Humanistic Instructional Paradigm
II.   Democratic Social Change
III. Self-Determined Evaluation
IV.   Confluent-Gestalt Model
V.   Transpersonal Orientation

Factor I, the *Humanistic Instructional Paradigm*, is dominated by the instructional value, "Individualism," which has the very high factor loading of .825, followed by eight other variables. This strongly suggests that these components, which make up the *most general model* of Confluent/Humanistic Education are led by the philosophy and teaching practices which encourage the kind of expressive individualism which also characterized the human potential movement.[3]

Factor II, second in the order of the power to explain the overall variance in this data, is termed *Democratic Social Change*. It indicates that most of us hold a democratically induced theory of social/ institutional change. Thus, our major theory of change is participative and we emphasize the three instructional values (see page 11) of "Context," "Innovation," and specifically "Democratic Participation" in the change process.

Factor III is very specific and refers to *Self-Determined Evaluation*. Evaluation is deemed to be very important in Confluent ideology *if* it is self-determined to the extent that this is practical.

Factor IV and V can be important in specific situations, even though

---

[2]Only 72.6% of the total variance was accounted for in these five factors. The remaining 27.4% of the variance was "splintered" into minor parts, too small to be described as substantively significant.

[3]In the "unrotated" factor loadings for principal components, there were 14 significant factor loadings (OTL Scales) in addition to "Individualism." Thus, all but the Transpersonal variable were included in this "Big Net," General Instructional Paradigm.

they are less powerful than the first three, in the sense of accounting for overall variance in the intercorrelation matrix from data derived from experts in Humanistic Education.

Factor IV can be termed the "Confluent-Gestalt Model" because *Integration* (of affect and cognition in instructional theory and practice) leads other components by a wide margin, followed by a less striking but still important consideration of *Relevance* (to the needs of the learners themselves and ultimately to the needs of society).

Factor V is termed the *Transpersonal Orientation.* This is the spiritual, "New-Age"-oriented set of beliefs which public school instruction presumably should include. An entire scale of this variable was constructed by this author and a colleague (Shapiro & Fitzgerald, 1989).

In summary, I regard the first three factors as comprising a major pattern or perspective from which we can observe and describe how Confluent Education is basically framed by experts in the field. These three factors, especially Factor I, form and support the *Humanistic Instructional Paradigm.* This essentially individualistic model is composed of a "big-net" (Factor I) supported by *Participatory Democracy* (Factor II) and *Self-Determined Evaluation* (Factor III). The *Confluent-Gestalt* and *Transpersonal Orientations* are secondary and assimilated into the more general paradigm.

3.   From verbatim statements in the writings of the experts, a 90 item Likert-type scale was developed, the Orientation to Learning (OTL). In one study it had a reliability of .892 (Shapiro, 1985b) and had presumably high face-validity via the sample selection itself. Table 1.1 presents a brief description of the 16 instructional values.

New "Orientation to Learning" Data

The following longitudinal data in Figure 1.1 had never been presented previous to the journal article on which this chapter is based. These are eight year-by-year mean overall Orientation to Learning scores (1983-90), produced by Confluent students along with comparable Counseling Psychology and Teacher Education scores over a shorter time span (1983-86) and (1983-85), respectively. The 1986 scores of a sample of Experienced Teachers ($N = 64$) are also included for comparative purposes.

Figure 1.1 reveals that the overall total mean scores of Confluent

Table 1.1

Brief Descriptions of the 16 Orientations to Learning Instructional Values

1. Process-Oriented: "How" is more important than "what" or "why." This orientation emphasizes "processing," talking over how an activity is being conducted and how it is being experienced.

2. Self-Determination: Includes autonomy, self-direction and self-evaluation. In this approach students assume initiative, responsibility and accountability whenever feasible and possible.

3. Connectedness: Encourages empathy, pluralism and good relationships. This approach is sometimes contrasted to individualism. Connectedness involves mutual caring and understanding among students and between student and teachers and others.

4. Relevance: This principle stresses the students' personal meanings and readiness to learn of the students. Instruction is related to underlying concerns and needs of the students as well as to society's interests.

5. Integration: In this approach affect is combined with cognition and "living" is combined with learning. Integration stresses educating the whole person including values, feelings and attitudes, the body, mind, and spirit of the learner.

6. Context: This includes awareness of the environment, culture, history and political and economic climate in which the learning takes place.

7. Affective-Bias: This is a preference for the use of feelings and concrete experience in learning. Instruction from this point of view also includes sensory awareness, immediate feelings and emotions and the expression of these as a central part of the learning experience.

8. Innovation: This is an anti-authoritarian, social and educational (systemic) orientation toward change. Innovation represents something new to the people engaged in learning and instruction intended to benefit those people and society.

(table continues)

9. Democratic Participation: This instructional value emphasizes social equity, consensus and collaboration in learning. Sometimes defined as "liberation," the process of full collaboration between students, teachers, other educational functionaries and the community determines how education shall take place.

10. Personal Growth: This principle stresses both methods and outcomes of learning as self-actualization through self-awareness. In this view, both the teacher and the learner, as persons, take precedence over the lesson plan, content, hardware or the "software" in education.

11. People-Oriented: People have intrinsic or ultimate value, not merely having instrumental importance as units or means of production. This approach to instruction shows trust in the learner's capacity to actualize him/herself. Learners, as other people, are basically hard-working, responsible, inherently good and naturally caring about one another.

12. Individualism: The person who is the learner is unique, self-determining and self-aware and is valued over the state or collective. What follows from this instructional and social principle is emphasis on personal freedom of expression, authentic self-hood and the individual is of ultimate concern in education.

13. Reality: This instructional value defines reality as concrete and pragmatic. True reality, therefore, "exists" as a given, objective condition. We can only know true reality by direct, primary feelings and experiences, not by fantasy or mental constructions. Reality is always based on the present—not the past or future.

14. Evaluation: "Formative" (using evaluation for growth and improvement) evaluation is favored over "summative" (final and additive number or stated rank summarizing and labeling a performance) evaluation. In formative evaluation the process is emphasized and quality is preferred to measures of quantity.

15. Variety and Creativity: This instructional approach values spontaneity, originality and diversity in the learning process. This is contrasted with conformity, standardization and preset goals for learning and growth. Flexibility and spontaneous exploration of feelings are encouraged.

(table continues)

16. Transpersonal (added in 1989): Schools and other settings for learning are environments for development of whole human beings and therefore include development of spiritual potential and mystical, intuitive and receptive modes as well as cognitive, rational, logical and active modes of consciousness.

students over the 8-year sample were very consistent (consistently higher than the other groups). Only in one year (1988) the overall mean Confluent scores significantly dropped, and in that year there were the fewest students ($N = 13$) admitted (versus 18.75 as the 8-year mean).

The 1988 group was qualitatively described by the Confluent faculty as being more reserved, cautious, introverted, and less spontaneous than those in the other years. But after one year in the program they began to appear much more like the usual, enthusiastic, expressive students. By the middle of the second year in the program, it was my impression that they were not perceived as different form the other Confluent cohorts.

Figure 1.1 indicates the typical scores for the Confluent students. Note that the typical OTL scores for Confluent students ($N = 150$) was near the *80th percentile* of the Graduate School of Education norm group ($N = 360$), derived from most of the programs in the School of Education.

The Counseling Psychology students varied from year to year around the *60th percentile* of the OTL and Teacher Education students usually scored around the *40th percentile*. As measured in 1986 only, Experienced Teachers in K-12, in the local public schools ($N = 55$), scored near the 20th percentile on the OTL. Table 1.2 indicates the data for the four programs illustrated in Figure 1.1 *within* the GSE to verify what appeared to be both statistical and substantive differences among these four programs. An analysis of differences and sources of differences were investigated.

To implement this analysis, recent advances in multilevel statistical techniques were employed (Kang, 1992; Raudenbush, 1988). These methods can provide estimates of how much the observed variance of aggregate measures are attributable to individual differences as contrasted with program differences.

Since not all program students were observed for the entire 8-year period, there are many missing cells, and the sample sizes differ across

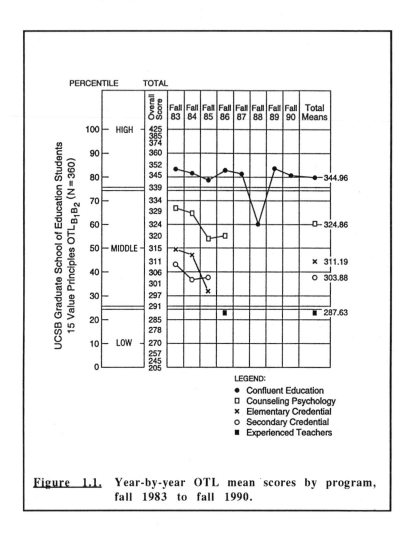

Figure 1.1. Year-by-year OTL mean scores by program, fall 1983 to fall 1990.

programs and across observation points of time. Kang's (1992) method enables investigators to make estimates of the values of the missing cells and, therefore, to compare other groups with Confluent students as the base.

Students in Confluent Education scored consistently higher than the students of other programs on their mean OTL scores and these differences are all highly significant ($p < .001$) even though the

Table 1.2

Overall Means and Variances of OTL Scores by Program (1983-1990 Inclusive)

Year		Confluent Education	Counseling Psychology	Elementary Credential	Secondary Credential	Row Total
				Program		
F 1983	M	349.12	330.31	314.34	310.45	327.23
	n	25	16	32	11	84
	Variance	1093.36	931.96	954.56	1293.27	1244.39
F 1984	M	346.69	328.14	312.41	302.00	318.18
	n	16	21	34	29	100
	Variance	772.90	1090.03	546.49	722.93	964.45
F 1985	M	343.62	319.29	298.27	303.22	317.26
	n	21	17	11	27	76
	Variance	1217.65	721.72	1431.02	1854.87	1631.80
F 1986	M	348.19	319.75			337.85
	n	21	12			33
	Variance	1122.96	613.48			1105.76
F 1987	M	346.05				346.05
	n	21				21
	Variance	2758.95				2758.95
F 1988	M	323.62				323.62
	n	13				13
	Variance	811.09				811.09
F 1989	M	349.53				349.53
	n	15				15
	Variance	591.98				591.98
F 1990	M	345.78				345.78
	n	18				18
	Variance	1716.65				1716.65
Column Total		344.96	324.86	311.19	303.88	326.42
		150	66	77	67	360
		1302.28	855.66	843.95	1242.29	1391.07

proportion of between-program variance to the total variance was only 17.5%. The observed mean differences among the four groups are substantial when the magnitude of the effects are considered.

Table 1.3 shows a ANOVA among six comparison groups on the OTL, with the years of measurement kept as simultaneous as possible. These ANOVAs and post hoc analyses show highly significant differences among *all* the major reference groups including Confluent Education, Counseling Psychology, Teacher Education, and Experienced Teachers. Not only are *all* the other groups distinguishable from Confluent Education students, they also are significantly different from one another, with the lone exception of the Elementary and Secondary Teaching candidates. Fully half of the Confluent students exceed the 73rd percentile, the 85th percentile, and the 94th percentile, respectively, of the students in Counseling, and Secondary and Elementary Student Teachers, and Experienced Teachers. This means that 73% of the Confluent students exceeded the mean scores of Counseling students, and exceeded the mean scores of 85% of Credential students, and 94% of Experienced Teachers, respectively.

If the OTL is generally and substantially reliable and valid (Shapiro, 1985a, 1985b, 1987, and the current study), Confluent Education students apparently comprise a very special kind of group insofar as instructional values are concerned. I infer from these studies that most Confluent educators really believe in these so-called humanistic education principles because the mean OTL scores are very high, above the so-called "upper-hinge" (75th percentile). Face and predictive validity on the OTL were established by written samples from the acknowledged experts and the confirmed predictions in the one-way ANOVA here and in previous studies. Construct validity was established in factor analyses (Shapiro, 1985a, 1985b, 1987, and current study) and concurrent validity in the correlations between the OTL and learning styles and the personality tests.

Year after year, the Confluent group scored the highest on the OTL, the Counseling Psychology students were next highest, followed by Teacher Credential students, and finally Experienced Teachers, who scored the lowest of all on the OTL. There was very little, if any, group overlap in the mean scores on this instrument.

What does all this mean? In my view this means that we were made up of a group of "true believers" when entering this program.

Table 1.3				
One Way ANOVA on Six Comparison Groups on the OTL				
Group	*n*	Year	Group Name	
1	42	F 85 & F 86	Confluent Education	
2	29	F 85 & F 86	Counseling Psychology	
3	45	F 84 & F 85	Elementary Credential	
4	56	F 84 & F 85	Secondary Credential	
5	40	F 86	High School (high or middle) Experienced Teachers	
6	24	F 86	Elementary Experienced Teachers	
Source ($N = 236$) *df*		SS	MS	F Ratio	F Prob.
Between Groups	5	93875.9147	18775.1829	15.2850	.00001
Within Groups	230	282517.7251	1228.3379		.0001
Total	235	376393.6398			

Moreover, when an alternate form of OTL B_1B_2 was administered at the end of the Spring Quarter 1984 after 1 year of exposure to the program, these scores were (statistically) significantly still higher than the original OTL scores at the beginning of the academic year of the program. In spite of the often found phenomenon of "regression to the mean," our people apparently became even more "true-believers" in the

Confluent/Humanistic doctrine (Shapiro, 1984). That doctrine will become more explicit later as this chapter proceeds.

This indicates to me that students begin this program as a self-selected, faculty-screened subgroup, literally a subculture, in the Graduate School of Education at UCSB. Apparently, we internalize these Confluent instructional values and, if anything, reinforce our original beliefs and maintain learning styles and personality features characteristic of this special subculture.

In a content analysis of 100 "pieces" representing the writings of experts in Humanistic Education (Shapiro, 1986), I found three principles which were endorsed most frequently. These, along with 13 other less prominent variables are now incorporated as subscales of the OTL. The "Big Three" are, in order of frequency, Affective Bias, Personal Growth, and Connectedness.

Affective Bias is a strong tendency to endorse awareness and expression of feelings and a somewhat anti-intellectual orientation. Personal Growth appears to be the major goal which is achieved by authentic expression of feelings in the context of warm, supportive small groups. Connectedness is the principle which embodies this kind of interaction.

These three instructional values account for 38.5% of all the 16 variables in this study, which provides another snapshot of the essence of Confluent Education: The expression of feelings in warm and authentic interpersonal settings is considered to generate personal growth and is endorsed as a very significant and legitimate object of learning.

In addition, more than a few studies (Shapiro, 1984, 1985a, 1985b, 1985c, 1986, 1987; Shapiro & Fitzgerald, 1989) add to this picture in the sense of the significant differences between Confluent Education students and other students in the UCSB Graduate School of Education and local public school teachers.

Since there was never any significant (statistical) difference found between the two credential groups, *four basic comparative groups* can be ordered below in terms of their *approximate* mean GSE percentile scores on the OTL over the sampling periods.

1. Confluent Education: 80th percentile
2. Counseling Psychology: 60th percentile
3. Teaching Credentials: 40th percentile
4. Experienced Teachers: 20th percentile

Each group is nearly evenly separated from each other group by 20 percentile points and these wide and evenly spaced differences appear to be clearly significant, statistically and substantively. The 20 percentile points differences are reflected on Table 1.3 through the Analysis of Variance (ANOVA), which reveals very significant overall differences (F, $15.285 = p < .0001$).

Personality Patterns and Learning Styles

In addition to the OTL and TOTL, administered over the 3-year period (1984-86), the Kolb Learning Styles Inventory (LSI) (Kolb, 1986) and the Kiersey Temperament Sorter (Kiersey & Bates, 1978) were given to Confluent and other students in the GSE. The "Kiersey" (K) is a short form of the total Myers-Briggs Type Indicator and highly correlated with it. The Myers-Briggs (MBTI) and the "Kiersey" measure *preferred* personality style or temperament.

It turns out that apparently here, again, the Confluent Program at UCSB attracts and selects a very special group of people. Table 1.4 reveals that a high percentage (80.0%) of Confluent people over the cohort period of testing (1984-1986 inclusive) in this sample prefer the "Intuitive Feeling" (NF) temperament. A chi-squared omnibus test shows significant differences among the four programs at the .05 level, and post-hoc analysis indicates that the Confluent Education group is significantly higher at the .05 level than the Counseling Psychology group and two Teacher Education Programs.

On the preferred temperament (measured by the Kiersey instrument) of the Confluent group over the entire period of testing (1984-1990 inclusive), the findings are that the modal personality pattern of Confluent students is slightly extroverted, strongly intuitive and feeling-oriented and indicates a slight preference for the function of Judgment (J) over Perception (P). So the modal Confluent temperament pattern is "ENFJ," dominated by "N and F" (Intuition and Feelings).

ENFJ, in Myers-Briggs terms, suggests proficient leaders of both task and growth groups. Characterized by Kiersey and Bates (1978) as having special charisma, they place a high value on cooperation, both from others and from themselves. They are often considered interpersonally adept, understanding, tolerant, appreciative, and skillful facilitators of effective communication. They are also noted for their

Table 1.4		
Percentage of "NFs" by Program on Kiersey Temperament Sorter Over 3-Year Period (1984-1986 Inclusive)		
Program	Percentage of "NFs"*	N
Confluent Education	80.0	60
Counseling Psychology	64.0	50
Elementary Teacher Education	56.5	69
Secondary Teacher Education	58.2	67
Mean (All Programs)/Total	64.2	246
*.05 level in omnibus chi-squared test.		

enthusiasm. On the negative side, apparently these people frequently feel responsible for the feelings of other people, which can place a burden on their interpersonal relations. Sometimes they find that others' demands overwhelm them, but most of the time they do not choose to protect themselves by withdrawal. Apparently, withdrawal and setting interpersonal limits are difficult for this group. Also, many people with the ENFJ pattern tend to idealize others and interpersonal relationships, with predictable consequences of disillusionment. Finally, they can also be vulnerable to inordinate guilt and self-criticism if they feel they let down people or their organization.

While only 31.5% of the actual Confluent group *exactly* fit this profile (about 5 to 6% in the general population, according to Kiersey and Bates), it remains the most typical personality pattern. The very large proportion of the NF temperament-types in Confluent/Humanistic groups indicates some variation in NF styles, but the central instructional values which emanate from NFs appear to be strikingly harmonious with the OTL data. In fact, this kind of temperament along with their preferred learning styles can be seen as a source of and support for the Confluent instructional principles advocated by this group on the OTL.

The above description reinforces the OTL-derived impression that we are a very select group. In effect, from the foregoing data, we can be described as an "NF subculture" (Intuitive-Feeling). NFs constitute only about 12% of the general population but approximately 40% of the GSE students. I also suspect that there are relatively far fewer faculty in the overall GSE with an NF temperament preference, whereas all four of the "academic ladder" Confluent faculty mentioned tested as "NFs."

Finally, with respect to the preferred learning style as measured by Kolb's LSI, the Confluent group is also quite different from the general population and the non-Confluent graduate students and professors at UCSB.

Of the four basic modes of learning, according to Kolb (1986), preference for learning (taking in) new information by one of these modes, "Concrete Experience" (CE), is noteworthy in the Confluent group. Learning by concrete experience involves direct and immediate sensory experience, touching, feeling, and contact with the "objects" of learning and experience.

Students in Confluent Education apparently strongly favor "Concrete Experience" as a primary mode of learning.[4] Confluent LSI scores were 82.7% concrete, whereas the Counseling Psychology group was only 63.8%. The comparable scores were 68.4% for Secondary Students and 64.8% for Elementary Students. Chi-squared tests show that these differences in the Confluent group are statistically significant at the .01 level.

Confluent students were approximately equally divided between action and reflection as favored modes of processing what has been grasped via concrete experience. Therefore, students in our group predominately prefer the learning styles of "Divergence" and "Accommodation," both of which are considered directly experienced and concrete as opposed to

[4]In Confluent Education, with most of its students there was, in my view, a widespread, implicit "learning contract," which was somewhat anti-intellectual, experiential, subjective, and constituted an affective bias, including a strong preference for "Concrete Experience" as *the* preferred learning mode. This made many Confluent student groups quite impatient with abstract conceptualization, theories and models which did not have immediate application (see p. 20).

abstract or conceptual.

It is important to note that "Divergent" learners most often major in the Helping Professions, Creative Arts and Humanities, and that "Accommodative" learners are often found in enterprising or entrepreneurial fields like business, sales, public relations, or advertising and are characterized as flexible and adaptive to the situation at hand. Extroverts are more likely to appear in the active learner-group and introverts in the more reflective group, but both groups probably would be receptive to techniques like Gestalt Awareness and experientially oriented groups. And indeed, empirical data derived from the OTL, LSI, and K instruments seem to confirm these preferences. (See Shapiro, 1985b, 1987.)

The relatively few people in the Confluent Program who were significantly different from the Confluent norms in temperament, learning style, or advocacy of Confluent/Humanistic instructional values, in my opinion, have also been valuable to this program because diversity has, to some extent, kept the Confluent students from what might have been an overwhelming affective and experiential bias. I think that there is always some group pressure for conformity, sometimes leading to a closed-thinking, self-sealing subculture. We needed the challenges of national, ethnic, gender, cultural and psychological diversity for viability in a rapidly changing society.

The Paradigmatic Basis of Confluent Education

Taking into consideration the Program's history, precursors, political forces, and quantitative data describing the students of Confluent Education, Table 1.5 lists five major themes (and sources of support), which presumably could form an overall paradigm of this approach to teaching, learning, and personal/professional development.

From Table 1.5 it can be seen that Confluent Education is and has been a subculture and a program with a definable philosophy and a coherent approach to instruction. These are substantially different from the academic premise(s) held by the surrounding *academic cultures* in the UCSB Department of Education, the Graduate School of Education, and the larger academic tradition of UCSB (and similar research-based universities).

Table 1.5

The Paradigmatic Basis of Confluent Education

Theme	Person-Centered	Holistic	Process-Oriented	Subjective	Developmental
Description	The locus of values centered on the growth of the person	Cognitive style, Epistemology is holistic	The preferred teaching -learning and functioning moves from Judging (J) to (P) Perceiving	Judgments about the inner and outer worlds based on subjective impressions.	Guiding theory, teaching and learning is developmental
Sources	Factor I, (NF) temperament, style, Self-determination, Relevance, Theory "Y" and Individualism. Concrete learning mode is strongly preferred to conceptual abstractions and theories	Factor II and III (N), Integration, Context, Personal Growth, Variety-Creativity and human context more important than academic disciplines per se	Process-oriented, Democratic Participation, Innovation Variety-Creativity, Factors I and III, Strong Preference for Divergent learning style.	Factor I, (F) on Myers-Briggs, Affect, Evaluation Reality, Personal Growth and Theory "Y". Preference for concrete/immediate experience to take in new information.	Factors I and III (NF) on Myers-Briggs, Innovation, Connected-ness, Personal Growth. Increase in affective complexity is major goal of learning.

The Confluent Subcultural Context
and Its Interpretation

The work of Edward T. Hall (1959, 1966, 1981, 1983), a cross-cultural, comparative anthropologist, provides a heuristic framework for interpreting the cultural paradigm, history, politics and nature of the norms and effects of Confluent Education on its teaching, learning, organizational, and personal/professional development. He laid the conceptual groundwork for a contextual aspect of cultures with his analysis and interpretation of two classically contrasting ways of dealing with time and space.

He termed these two approaches monochronic (one-at-a-time) and polychronic (many-things-at-the-same-time). The people in monochronic cultures are described by him as low-involvement. They typically segment and compartmentalize both time and space. They usually schedule only one activity or one person at a time *because* they tend to become disoriented if they have to cope with too many things simultaneously within the same space. In addition, activities and interactions are assigned to their "proper spaces" within "appropriate" physical/architectural structures. These are basic features of a so-called low-context culture.

Polychronic people tend to be very involved with one another, often keep several operations (and sets of people) going simultaneously (like jugglers). Unlike the incumbents of monochronic cultures, the polychronic people do not seem to need to separate activities in space. Many functions go on in the same space. The "proper" ordering of time and space does not appear to be nearly as important to polychronic people as it does to those within a monochronic cultural context. As depicted in Table 1.6, Hall closely correlates monochronic cultures as being low in context and polychronic cultures as having a high context.

High-context cultures emphasize background whereas low-context cultures emphasize foreground, the immediate specific "messages," without much awareness of or attention to the connotative meanings of the communications. Table 1.6 elaborates these differences in terms of conceptions of time, space, interpersonal relations, wholeness, change, and central values related to "production" versus "people."

In summary, I regard us as attempting to develop a relatively high-context subculture surrounded by a hierarchy of low-context subcultures typical of research-based universities, the community of Santa Barbara

Table 1.6

Low- and High-Context Cultural Features

	Low-Context Cultures	High-Context Cultures
Examples	USA, Switzerland, No. Germany	Iran, Latin America, Native-American, the Orient, and Russia
Concept of Time	Monochronic:	Polychronic:
	One thing at a time. Time-ridden, obsession with time, Promptness highly valued, short-term perspective.	Many things simultaneous. Not clock or time-bounded. Appointments treated casually, longer term perspective.
	Time, like a material/tangible resource can be spent, earned, served, wasted, used, etc.	Time proceeds, passes in "natural" succession (e.g., Holidays, ceremonies, even business begins and ends with the "new moon" and the "old moon.")
	Time is segmented, scheduled, discrete, compartmentalized. Metaphors for time are linear, (road, path, ribbon)	Time is like a museum with endless alcoves and corridors.
Space	Activities and people separated in space as well as time.	Many roles, activities, people within the same space. Toleration of high density population.
Relationships, Contacts, and Communication	Highly individualistic. People alienated, separated, esp. from different class, age, ethnicity. People become more and more like their machines. Information is hoarded and privileged.	People generally deeply involved with others. Relationships and community more important than time, production, efficiency. Information is widely shared. High sensory input and involvement.
Wholeness	Culture fragmented, not whole or integrated "War of the parts vs. the whole"	Culture widely shared, relatively integrated, not compartmentalized.
Change	Can absorb technical extensions without much systemic change. Preoccupation with *change* in people, things, technology and in *overcoming* resistance to change.	Can't easily absorb mechanical extensions without losing cultural integrity. Often tradition-oriented. Basic change in culture usually very difficult.
Production Values vs. Tradition of Interpersonal Bonding	Business "know how" substituted for tradition. Tradition limited mainly to a benchmark for technical progress/development. OK to do business with strangers.	Business/production often mixed with personal/interpersonal exchanges of information and social "visiting". Business with strangers usually difficult.

California, and the USA in general.

The paradigmatic basis of Confluent Education (Person-Centered, Holistic, Process-Oriented, Subjective, and Developmental), noted in Table 1.5 maps nicely onto the features of High-Context Cultures indicated in Table 1.6.

The one prominent low-context cultural feature in the Confluent subculture, however, is "Individualism." This is part of the "Person-Centered" theme in the Confluent paradigm. This appears to be a deep contradiction because "Individualism" had by far the highest factor loading in the "rotated" analysis of experts' views. This anomaly is also precisely the value most often criticized by sophisticated observers of the Human Potential Movement and Humanistic Psychology, key precursors of Humanistic Education. (See Bellah et al., 1985; Friedman, 1992; Koch, 1971; Plumb, 1993; Smith, 1991; and many other highly regarded scholars.)

However, a crucial distinction between "Expressive Individualism" and "Utilitarian Individualism" is made explicit only by Bellah and his colleagues, who, along with de Tocqueville, regard excessive individualism as a deep flaw in American culture.

I contend that the Confluent subculture was characterized by Expressive ("warm") Individualism much more than "Utilitarian ("cool") Individualism. This is supported by the preferred personality pattern ("NF") and the significantly "Concrete" (expressive) learning style of most of the Confluent students.

In spite of the above disclaimers, however, it is my opinion that the kind of Expressive Individualism evidenced in the unorthodox teaching styles and research issues of the professors and students in the Confluent subculture was precisely what alienated us from the surrounding low-context academic subculture. Most academics would not have objected to the Utilitarian Individualism underlying their own enterprise.

Finally, I do regard our individualism as a mixed blessing. The consequences of our individualism contained the same implicit paradox which ultimately led to a decline of the Human Potential Movement (according to Plumb, 1993) and of Humanistic Psychology (according to Friedman, 1992). In nearly all other respects, however, I still note our *attempt* to create a relatively higher context academic subculture than other academic programs. In most ways, we did succeed in that mission, eventually at the cost of our own survival as a viable program in the Education Department at UCSB. The humanistic instructional values of the Confluent students and professors and their controversial political position within the Education Department at UCSB and across the campus can be interpreted as essentially a clash of cultures.

Conclusions

The ultimate dissolution of Confluent Education as a distinct and separate program for M.A.s and Ph.D.s and other graduate students occurred when it was merged with the program of Educational Policy Organizations and Leadership (EPOL) to form the new Educational Leadership and Organizations (ELO) program within the Education Department of the Graduate School of Education (fall 1992).

This merger was alleged to include some of the experiential interpersonal and small-group aspects of Confluent Education, but that is quite doubtful because the search committee has concluded its fourth search for a replacement for one of the retired senior professors in Confluent Education. The position has been partially saved, but the confluent emphasis is gone. The recent retirements of the three major (senior) professors actually marked the deconstruction of Confluent Education as an academic program. In my view, most of the elements of the "Confluent Paradigm" and its relatively high-context subculture have been and will continue to be "merged out of existence."

In the fall of 1992 no new Confluent students were admitted and although a few types of confluent courses were still being taught as of the spring of 1994 (e.g., Group Dynamics, Small-Group Leadership and Organizations, and Interpersonal Relations), they were taught by part-time instructors. Confluent Education as a program or emphasis no longer exists. Most of the few remaining Confluent students are in the "pipeline" and the majority of them are expected to graduate from M.A. or Ph.D. programs within the next few years.

Without the protective function of the three retired or retiring senior professors, who had significant political and academic influence, and with diminishing or threatened economic fortunes in the University and the State of California, the enclave of a high-context, confluent subculture was no longer sustainable in an essentially low-context, research-dominated academic environment.

True, there are a number of significant "offsprings" of this movement, which will be documented in Chapter 4, The Legacy of

Confluent Education. Among the most evident are in the Elementary
Teaching Credential Program at UCSB, and with some now-accepted
practices in the public schools under different labels. There is the
highly innovative, private, alternative Santa Barbara Middle School, and
the outstanding local example of a free-standing graduate school
significantly influenced by the Confluent model. The latter is the
Pacifica Graduate Institute in the Santa Barbara area.

But perhaps the greatest institutional impact of this program has been
in Norway, with relatively many schools, colleges, universities and
personal/professional programs and centers which are at least partly
based on confluent principles. This is largely due to the extensive
"missionary" work of George and Judith Brown, the late Nils Magnar
Grendstadt, Rolf-Petter Larsen, Jostein Cleveland, Olaf-Martin Lund,
and others too numerous to mention here. I also include myself in this
group. Whether similar "confluent" manifestations of the still active,
now world-wide but dispersed, Human Potential Movement can survive
within a low-context academic subculture still remains open to
conjecture.

Chapter 2

The Origins of Confluent Education

It was my intention in the first chapter to provide some basic but somewhat localized and, therefore, limited material for understanding both the essence and demise of the Confluent Education Program. However, to more deeply understand this program as a product of far greater and more complex forces, I think it is necessary to examine its *historical* origins.

As with the study of many other broadly based programs, it is difficult to know where to start and when to stop when considering the origins of Confluent Education. This chapter cannot do justice to the many movements, influences, people, programs, and institutions which have, in some way, contributed to the origination and development of Confluent Education. Some of these influences are obvious, direct, and recent but apparently there are significant roots and connections which are relatively remote in time, complex, and indirect. Furthermore, there are several well informed sources for the origins and influences on what Brown (1971) called "affective education" and/or "psychological education." These approaches originally were synonyms for Confluent Education in the early stages of its development (1966-1971). Later, Confluent Education attempted to separate and elevate itself into a "genus," significantly different from these similar species of education.

This chapter will be my attempt to identify themes and foundations rather than to provide a complete historical summary. I am not a trained historian nor philosopher, but nevertheless, I will attempt here to identify what I have found as the major origins within this complex field in order to further clarify the nature of modern Confluent Education and how it arrived at its present state in 1998. The inherent difficulty of this task is confirmed by Wertz (1992, p. 474).

Also, I have not found in the literature I have surveyed anything like a serious and sustained presentation of the philosophical, social, and psychological foundations of Confluent Education. There are several impressive histories of Humanistic Education, and the philosophical and psychological foundation of Humanistic Psychology from which I have liberally drawn. Some of the most prominent of these sources include C. H. Patterson's *Humanistic Education* (1973); H. Misiak's and V. S. Sexton's *Phenomenological, Existential and Humanistic Psychologies: A Historical Survey* (1973); J. R. Royce's and L. P. Mos' *Humanistic Psychology: Concepts and Criticisms* (1981); a special issue of the *Humanistic Psychologist*, "The Humanistic Movement in Psychology" (1992), F. J. Wertz (Guest Ed.); and E. L. Simpson's *Humanistic Education: An* Interpretation (1976).

Additional sources are from the Association for Supervision and Curriculum Development, *A New Look at Progressive Education*, prepared by the ASCD 1972 Yearbook Committee, J. R. Squire (Ed.); *Four Psychologies Applied to Education: Freudian, Behavioral, Humanistic and Transpersonal*, T. B. Roberts (Ed.) (1975); and Corliss Lamont's *The Philosophy of* Humanism (1982).

That most of these appeared in the 1970s I have found significant. This period of proliferation included Humanistic Psychology, Humanistic Education, the Human Potential Movement, the so-called counter-culture, and the Encounter Group Movement, and descriptions of many similar programs to liberate people and to help them "actualize their potential."

Figure 2.1 is a flow chart of the origins of Confluent Education. While I recognize that no linear chart can capture the nuances of the various zeitgeists and nonlinear connections among the various components, I found that I needed a map to organize my records and observations of this "hard-to-define" enterprise. I present this flow chart at least as much for my own need for structure as for the reader's understanding of a movement with so many forbearers.

From Aristotle to Confluent Education

For the early Greeks, especially Aristotle, the purpose of education was to develop good citizens. Athens emphasized freedom and personal development and encouraged the individual development of one's physical, psychological, and artistic capabilities. *Arete* (excellences) included intellectual as well as moral excellence.

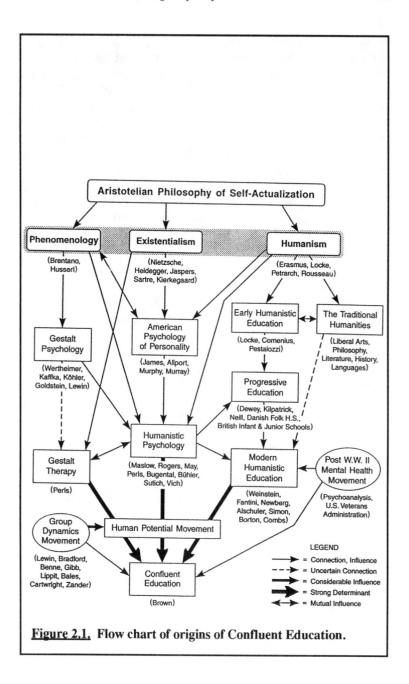

Figure 2.1. Flow chart of origins of Confluent Education.

Aristotle was, according to Patterson (1973, p. 33), "a humanist and to the virtue of intellect or reason he added those of the practical, the artistic and the moral." Education was to him an internal process, assisted by external agents, in which the individual actualized his potentialities. The ultimate goal of all human striving is self-actualization. Happiness is desirable for its own sake, as the ultimate goal. The ultimate aim of education is the attainment of happiness and depends, in man, on both individual and cooperative efforts. In Europe, learning was to be a life-long activity. Quoting from Patterson,

> Aristotle influenced many of those who later wrote about education, including Erasmus, Petrarch, Pestalozzi, Comenius, Locke, and Rousseau. Unfortunately, the ideas of Locke, Rousseau, and Pestalozzi had very little influence on the philosophy or education of their times or immediately afterwards. Authoritarian discipline and memorization dominated education to the extent that Comenius called the schools "the slaughter-houses of the mind. (1973, pp. 43-44)

Aristotle's ideas (384-322 BC), generated approximately 23 1/2 centuries ago, reemerged during the 12th century in Arab lands and the Latin West. Slowly his philosophy of self-actualization was reconciled with Christianity and became the principal subject matter of higher education from the 13th to the 17th century in England. This education contributed to the rise of neoclassicism and, as such, left its mark especially on English and Western European philosophy and literature (poetry, drama, essays, biographies, and politically-oriented works).

As mentioned above, some of the most prominent figures were Erasmus (Noll & Kelly, 1970a); Locke (Gay, 1964); Petrarch (Jarrett, 1973); and Rousseau (Frankel, 1947). Comenius (Noll & Kelly, 1970b); Pestalozzi (Gutek, 1968); and Locke (Gay, 1964) began what I have termed Early Humanistic Education.

According to Patterson (1973), these scholar/educators were some of the remote ancestors of Modern Humanistic Education, including Confluent Education. Among many well-known philosophical Humanists were Erasmus, Locke, Petrarch, and Rousseau. Phenomenology was probably originated by Brentano and later led by Husserl (1925/1962, 1965). Phenomenology strongly stimulated the development of Gestalt Psychology, in which the leading figures were Wertheimer (1912/1965), Koffka (1935), Köhler (1929), Goldstein

(1940), and Lewin (1952).

The third main tributary of philosophy which nourished the American Psychology of Personality was Existentialism (Misiak & Sexton, 1973, pp. 68-106). The first two were Phenomenology and the philosophy of Humanism (Lamont, 1982) (see Figure 2.1). The Danish religious scholar Soren S. Kierkegaard (1941, 1944) was allegedly the original inspiration of the philosophy of Existentialism. His original work was written almost 100 years before being published in English (Royce & Mos, 1981, p. 58). It strongly influenced Existentialism, especially the work of Martin Heidegger, who broke away from his immediate phenomenological mentor, Edmund Husserl (1965).

Although Heidegger succeeded Husserl as Chair of Philosophy at the German University of Freiberg, the former's philosophy radically departed from Phenomenology and became largely responsible for the emergence of Existentialism in the late 1920s (see Heidegger, 1962, 1977).

Nietzsche (1883-92) was also a German existialist philosopher who continually tried to penetrate to the irrational level of existence beneath earlier systematic, rational philosophy. (See Barrett, 1958.)

Two other important European leaders in philosophical Existentialism were Sartre (1943, 1947, 1953) and Jaspers (1954, 1957), whose contributions to the field of Existential psychology and therapy and to the American Psychology of Personality will be discussed later in this chapter.

Phenomenology, Existentialism, and Humanism were and are part of what is known as Modernism, which blossomed in the second half of the 19th century in the Western world. Modernism was based on the collapse of certainty and the failure of many old verities in Western culture. Western culture was founded on Judeo-Christian belief systems which were profoundly shaken by a series of attacks. The sources of these attacks were from paradigmatic changes in science, philosophy, and anthropology. Phenomenology, Existentialism, and Humanism were the major sources of the American Psychology of Personality, all of which emphasized inner awareness, subjectivity, irrationality, and relativism. These changes represented a repudiation of the almost total religious domination of Western culture and society in the Middle Ages.

The Early Roots of Humanistic Philosophy and Education

As mentioned above, Erasmus, Locke, Petrarch, and Rousseau, though separated by over a century and a half, are considered key figures in the philosophy of Humanism (Patterson, 1973, p. 34). The term "humanism" was applied to their philosophy near the end of the 15th century. These philosophers were *also educators* (this author's emphasis), who were concerned with the liberal arts and literature and the association with what became known as the humanities, based on the Greek and Latin classics as subject matter.

"Renaissance Humanism" was *primarily* a revolt against medieval Christianity, especially in the latter's emphasis on God, Christ, Heaven, and immortality. The ideal man became "Renaissance Man," the universal man, with a many-sided personality, joy in living, and delighting in all kinds of earthly achievements (Lamont, 1982, p. 20). The most important outcome of early Humanism was its help in emancipating people from the religious control of knowledge which characterized the Dark Ages.

Erasmus (Noll & Kelly, 1970a), one of the earliest of this group emphasized virtue, character, and intelligence rather than dogma or authority. John Locke was an English philosopher who strongly influenced Thomas Jefferson and other early American statesmen. His central contributions were a humane respect for the child as an individual and his humanitarian view that the individual does not exist for the state. Individuals, he believed, were "human beings of worth" (Patterson, 1973, p. 37). Petrarch was considered by some scholars (e.g., Siepmann, 1987, pp. 755-756) to be the "first humanist" or the first "modern man." He was an itinerant Italian poet and philosopher, as well as devout Christian, who helped to reconcile ancient Greek philosophy with Christianity in the 14th century. Jean Jacques Rousseau (1762/1947) was strongly influenced by both Aristotle and Locke and focused on learners as "naturally good" (Patterson, 1973, p. 38), and proclaimed in his writings that education should follow the inclinations of human nature. For him, the key was becoming a human being, true to *his own nature* (this author's emphasis), *in* (this author's emphasis) the world but *not* (this author's emphasis) of it. This is very close to the modern concept of "self-actualization" and was also very congruent with many of Aristotle's and Locke's positions.

In view of the above, although I find it very difficult to separate

Philosophical Humanists from early Humanistic educators, I include John Amos Comenius and Johann H. Pestalozzi in this latter, distinguished group noted in Figure 2.1.

Comenius (Noll & Kelly, 1970b) proposed a system of progressive instruction adjusted to the developmental stage of the child and this was, according to Piaget (1967, p. 10), a precursor of the genetic idea in child psychology. Comenius advocated learning by experience and by doing (see Dewey, 1929, p. 22) before generalizations or rules were given and insisted that the subject matter and experiences were to be relevant to the needs of the child. He also emphasized the familiar concepts of emphasis on sense perception and experience (similar to Phenomenology, Gestalt Psychology, Existentialism, Gestalt Therapy, and Confluent Education).

Pestalozzi (Gutek, 1968), born in Switzerland like Rousseau, built upon the insights of Comenius and Rousseau. As with the latter two educational philosophers, Pestalozzi focused on the total development of the child, and regarded education as based on the "child's natural development" (Patterson, 1973, p. 41). However, Pestalozzi was more specifically concerned with the details of learning and instruction, especially with poor children, as contrasted with Rousseau's focus on the children of well-to-do parents.

In addition to the above specifics, Pestalozzi was primarily an educator rather than a philosopher as were Locke and Rousseau. The former stressed the rights of each person to develop his potentialities and the duty to allow other men the same freedom. Thus, Pestalozzi, even more than Erasmus, Locke, Rousseau, and Comenius, endorsed education for self-actualization in what later became the core of the Human Potential Movement in which I presume Confluent Education is deeply involved. (See Figure 2.1.)

Pestalozzi provided a strong link between early Humanistic Education and Progressive Education in Europe and later in America under the leadership of John Dewey—the central philosopher/educator in the latter movement. Like Dewey, Pestalozzi emphasized learning by direct experience or as Dewey put it, "learning by doing." Finally, Pestalozzi also centered on providing a strongly humanistic, supportive atmosphere/context for learning, very similar to that of Modern Humanistic Education, including Confluent Education. The end result of these concerns was the generation of "fully-functioning" (Rogers, 1985) or "self-actualizing" (Maslow, 1968) learners.

Thus it can be seen that the origins of Humanistic Education are at least 23 1/2 centuries old, beginning with Aristotle and after a long quiescent stage in the Dark Ages, moving with Erasmus, Locke, Rousseau, Comenius, and Pestalozzi, and others too numerous to mention. For all of these outstanding scholars, the goal of education was not exclusively the development of a scholar or a "good" citizen of a state but on becoming integrated, balanced, whole persons. It appears that the foundations of Humanistic Education were clearly laid out, beginning almost 500 years ago. Therefore, according to these considerations, Confluent Education, along with Modern Humanistic Psychology and Education, can be characterized by their "embeddedness" in humanistic politics, religion, history, philosophy, psychology, and education. We *did not* (this author's emphasis) spring fully formed as Athena is said to have "from the head of Zeus." Nor did we "just 'growed' like Topsy" in *Uncle Tom's Cabin.*

The Uncertain Connection Between the Traditional Humanities and Modern Humanistic Education

Figure 2.1 indicates that the "Traditional Humanities" came originally from the rediscovery of the classics and later from the broad philosophy of Humanism, beginning in the Renaissance, in the early 14th century in Europe and later in more intellectual/scientific terms in the Enlightenment, beginning late in the 17th century. But to what degree are the traditional humanities, including liberal arts, philosophy, literature and language, and possibly some aspects of history, connected with Modern Humanistic Education/Psychology? This is the question Jarrett (1973) asks in Chapter 8, p. 105 in his work *The Humanities and Humanistic Education.* As previously mentioned, Elizabeth Leone Simpson (1976) states:

> I argue at length below that "humanistic" as a broad rubric includes such *separate* (this author's emphasis) educational developments as confluent education, affective education, self-as-science, and psychological education.
>
> I further argue that humanistic education as I construe it has deep roots in and affinities with the traditional humanities. Because some of the cherished values of the humanities find a reflection and embodiment in humanistic education, this is, in fact, the statement of a significant relationship. (p. 1)

Since Humanistic Education, according to both Jarrett and Simpson, is very umbrella-like in its ambiguity and has many definitions and practices and is a "broad rubric," including various and separate forms, for me the cogent biological metaphor for use becomes "genus" rather than "species." There are a multiplicity of labels and synonyms for Humanistic Education (e.g., Affective Education, Psychological Education, Experiential Education, Value-Free Education, Integrated Learning, Confluent Education). Also, it appears to be notoriously difficult to define, especially in the form of Confluent Education. (See this chapter, pp. 38-39 and Chapter 3, pp. 97-98.)

Simpson (1976, p. 2) considers awareness of affect and its expression as central to Humanistic Education and cites its three foci:

1.   The feelings that grow out of the content of the curriculum itself and the relevance of the issues it presents to the lives of the learners.
2.   The preconditions of learning, those feelings of acceptance and competence, reinforced by a supportive environment, so that the context of learning leads to self-esteem.
3.   Feelings as the content of curricula. This involves personal/emotional material which students bring to class regardless of whether they are handled directly, individually, or in a group, like encounter groups or supports groups, application of Gestalt techniques or creative arts.

In spite of Simpson's claim of the *essential* (this author's emphasis) affinities of Humanistic Education with the traditional disciplinary humanities, she reveals her ambivalence toward this relationship (pp. 5-7) when she states:

The claims of the humanities to be considered humanistic education are not to be casually dismissed, but neither are these disciplines to be automatically included. The substance of a classical humanities curriculum need not necessarily lead to a humanistic education. . . . (pp. 5-6)

Simpson (1976) admits that the affective/personal components of the humanities may not translate into concrete, authentic humanistic experience and that the total domain of these two broad fields are different (p. 6). According to her, however, [and this reflects some of the same ambivalence of Jarrett] "What binds contemporary humanistic studies [what I have labeled as "Modern Humanistic Education" in Figure 2.1] to the traditional humanities is concern, not just with man's highest values, but also with those values as uniquely the product of passion as well as of intellect of emotion as well as reason" (p. 6).

Jarrett (1973, pp. 106-107) further reveals the sources of his ambivalence in that he perceives "a discernible spread" in the uses of the term "humanistic." He is referring to a continuum among contemporary educators and psychologists ranging from individualistic psychology and ethics to the more "sociological and political way of thinking about and reforming institutions (such as schools and school systems), communities, and whole nations and societies."

Further, in addition to the now familiar definitional problems, he states that humanistic educators and psychologists need not see the study of the humanities as helpful in their cause:

> Indeed they might even see the humanities as elitist, as symbols of inequality in society and social justice or (p. 107) even as an opiate of the people. Furthermore, they *may* [emphasis by Jarrett] be uninterested in religion, philosophy, or the arts and the kinds of values mainly associated with such endeavors. Contrariwise, the devotee of the humanities *may* [emphasis by Jarrett] be himself aristocratic, snobbish, even tyrannical. (Jarrett, 1973, pp. 106-107)

Working through various definitions of religious humanism, Renaissance humanism, humanitarianism, humanistic psychology and the humane, Jarrett (1973) arrives close to Simpson's position (1976) in his conclusion that both the study of the humanities and Humanistic Education/Psychology, in the last analysis, involve:

1. Richly valuative responses.
2. Capacity for deep subjectivity, along with heightened sensibilities, intellect and knowledge.
3. Involving a large portion of ourselves as feeling, personal beings as well as inquirers and knowers.
4. The same enduring object: the enlargement of the human spirit.
(p. 111)

Interpreting the foregoing observations (especially the ambivalence and the definitional complexities), I come away with a feeling/perception of some basic common elements. However, in my opinion, there are neither necessary nor sufficient conditions for a direct relationship. These two important traditions have an uncertain relationship with one another in the network of origins of Confluent Education. (See Figure 2.1 with the dotted lines on the right side of the Flow Chart.)

Progressive Education

In Figure 2.1, Progressive Education is seen as an intervening movement between early and Modern Humanistic Education. This position between early and modern stages of humanism applied to schools was briefly discussed above in connection with Comenius' and Pestalozzi's emphasis on learning by experience (by doing) and, therefore, provide a link between early Humanistic Education and Progressive Education from 1918 to the present (ASCD Yearbook, 1972, *A New Look at Progressive Education*, edited by James R. Squire; and Darling, 1994). The years from 1918 through the 1930s were apparently the zenith of Progressive Education.

According to Loving (1972, pp. v-vi),

> If progressive education had successfully broken through the barrier of traditional education during the thirties and forties, perhaps we would avoided most of the social unrest of the 1960s and 1970s.

His major point, I think, was that Progressive Education was the flagship for each stage of democratic development, from understanding each child as a unique human being to understanding "our ever-changing society."

That Progressive Education's central figure was John Dewey, one of America's foremost philosophers and educators, appears to be confirmed from many sources (e.g., Lamont, 1982; Patterson, 1973; Squire, 1972; Darling, 1994) as well as the many works by Dewey himself (e.g., Dewey, 1900/1956, 1902, 1916/1926, 1922, 1929, 1938). Since so many publications already describe and eulogize his theories and their practical effects on education, I will attempt here to focus on the important connections of Progressive Education with Modern Humanistic Education, the Human Potential Movement and, ultimately, Confluent Education itself.

According to Lamont (1982, p. 22), Dewey and, therefore,

Progressive Education belong to what is called *Naturalistic Humanism* (this author's emphasis), a world-view in which nature is reality and in which there is no supernatural and man is an integral part of nature and not separated from it, despite all that remains to be discovered about nature. This is at odds, intellectually, with "borderline" connections between Confluent Education and Psychosynthesis, for example, with its concept of a Higher (spiritual) Self (see Yoemans, 1975a, 1975b and note his deep interest in Psychosynthesis and spiritual [transpersonal] psychology). It is also noteworthy that in the later OTL studies, a separate identifiable variable was identified (i.e., transpersonal orientation) in the writings of humanistic educators and psychologists and a separate instrument, the TOTL, was constructed by myself and Louise F. Fitzgerald (Shapiro & Fitzgerald, 1989). Despite the above connections with spirituality, which borders on supernatural beliefs, I think that Confluent Education remained largely pragmatic and secular (see Iannaccone, 1996, p. 173).

John Dewey apparently recognized the implications of Darwin's *Origin of the Species* (1859/1956) and rejected the doctrine of supernatural forces and entities and was thus classified as a pragmatist, following the lead of William James. This was despite the latter's inclination toward the subjective, mystical orientation which confused the secular humanists and pragmatists.

Among the many connections between Dewey's and A. S. Neill's Progressive Education to Modern Humanistic Education and Confluent Education are the instructional values of personal growth, participatory democracy, self-determination, variety-creativity, individualism, affective expression, and innovation. The concept of the primacy of experience and process-orientation as the central focus for education sounds like the "reality principle" of Humanistic and Confluent Education. Perhaps the clearest exposition of the overall Humanistic Education Paradigm which I found in my multivariate factor analyses of the OTL is expressed in Progressive Education terms as follows:

> The cultivation of individuality, a cornerstone of progressive education, is a conceptual meeting place for the moral, social and scientific focus of progressivism. . . . One hundred years of study have contributed the most controversial set of facts relevant to education—that each individual is biologically, socially and psychologically unique. (Squire, 1972, p. 3)

In the Dewey School at the University of Chicago and subsequent other merged schools in Chicago, the primary skills in reading, writing, and numbers were to grow out of true needs of the children and the results of shared activities. It was a "self-contained" classroom (see Squire, 1972, pp. 131-132). For the details of the "activity programs" which characterized Progressive curricula see Squire (1972, pp. 214-216).

Although the progressive movement in American education is often associated with John Dewey, perhaps the most influential introducer of progressive ideas into American schools was William Heard Kilpatrick. His books and articles (1918, 1926, 1930, 1933) were used as key educational texts.

At Teachers College, Columbia University, he directly trained a large number of future education professors in the formative years, 1918-1940 (Hirsch, 1996, p. 52). Kilpatrick placed wholehearted, purposeful activity at the core of curriculum construction. Apparently, he conceived individual purposeful activity as the key to educational experience (Kilpatrick, 1918, p. 320). Such activity, as it proceeded through the essential steps of purposing, planning, executing, and judging, brought learners to content, intrinsic to the enterprise. Also, Kilpatrick projected the purposive act into a social environment in collaborative coping with a variety of situations which could enhance ethical relationships.

Apparently, educational revolutionaries, like Dewey and Kilpatrick, sponsored a philosophy of child growth, which included freedom, activity, initiative, responsibility, and the integration of personality. Kilpatrick specifically disputed what was called the "scientific study" of the child because it dealt with fragments of knowledge, separate skills, separate habits, and seemed to forget personality altogether.

Summerhill

Patterson (1973) considers A. S. Neill's Summerhill the best known example of Humanistic Education at the time, although I have classified it in Figure 2.1 as part of Progressive Education. In truth, I think it is a primary example of both movements because they are so closely related yet different enough to identify because of their various approaches to actual curricula and instruction, while being very similar in educational philosophy.

Summerhill was probably the most radical attempt to facilitate learning as natural development in an atmosphere of love, responsibility, freedom, and understanding. It was the creation of A. S. Neill (1960) and founded in England in 1921. It was coeducational and extended from age 4 to 18 years. The students lived in group homes with about 45-50 students, each headed by a housemother.

The focus at Summerhill (Popenoe, 1970) was the total development of the child. Academic/intellectual development was considered secondary to emotional development, but the students were restricted by the need to meet society's requirements and its institutions for credits, courses, and certification (e.g., diplomas). Attendance at classes was optional but, over time, most students developed strong motivation to attend the classes and other activities.

Summerhill epitomizes many of the Humanistic Education instructional values, such as connectedness, expression of affect as well as ideas and perceptions, self-determination, individualism, process orientation, within a context of social responsiveness, personal growth, and self-evaluation. Its alleged success was held to be due to the kinds of people who are the staff and, especially, the context/atmosphere of respect, understanding, patience, relevance, basic humanity, and even love. As such, it remains a powerful model of Humanistic Education— and, indeed, Progressive Education (Patterson, 1973, p. 49).

The Danish Folk High School

Another outstanding model for Progressive Education are the Danish Folk High Schools which began in 1910 (Davis, 1971, p. 6). This Folk High School Movement was intended to help the common young man (age 18 years or more) to learn his own value and nourishing this with Denmark's past and mother tongue when the languages of the educated classes were Latin and German. This institution is supported by the government and students are supported on the basis of financial need.

It is believed that the Folk High Schools have raised the level of literacy in Denmark, as well as fostering cooperation and civic participation. With the freedom to attend or not and a curriculum deliberately constructed to fit the needs of students and teachers, this model of Progressive Education also fits closely with Modern Humanistic and Confluent Education which developed later in America.

British Infant and Junior Schools

Summerhill was criticized as too extreme in de-emphasizing academic/intellectual development and for not being very applicable to nonresidential schools. The British Infant and Junior Schools incorporated many aspects of Summerhill in a nonresidential and more academically oriented way (Plowden Report, 1967; Silberman, 1970, p. 209).

Resembling a modern American kindergarten, these British schools are hives of activity of various kinds, all happening at once. This is a noteworthy example of a high context culture according to E. T. Hall (1981, 1983). These schools are not teacher-dominated. Children are respected and the school experience is considered important in itself, not simply as preparation for the future (Patterson, 1973, p. 52). This feature also epitomized the modern humanistic instructional value of process-orientation.

The role of the teacher is to actively facilitate the processes in which the children are engaged, and thus this exemplifies Child-Centered Education described in detail by Darling (1994). According to Silberman (1970, p. 228),

> What impresses the American observer the most, however, is the combination of great joy and spontaneity and activity with equally great self-control and order. The joyfulness is pervasive: in almost every classroom visited, virtually every child appeared happy and engaged. One simply does not see bored or restless or unhappy youngsters or youngsters with the glazed look so common in American schools. The joy is matched by an equally impressive self-discipline and relaxed self-confidence. There seems not to be any disruptive youngsters in informal classrooms—indeed, few of the behavior problems with which American teachers are almost always coping.

The informal English Infant and Junior Schools demonstrate in practice what Dewey argued in theory: that a deep and genuine concern for individual growth and fulfillment demands an equally genuine concern for cognitive growth, and intellectual disciplines. This not only indicates that they are excellent examples of Progressive Education but it further underlines the key Humanistic/Confluent instructional value of the integration of cognitive and affective experience in the process of learning.

Thus, it can be seen that Progressive Education models involve an environment characterized by a humanistic and often high-context subculture. Modern Humanistic Education, on the other hand, relies more on specific interventions as in Self-Science, Values Clarification, a Curriculum of Affect and Gestalt techniques in the classroom. Indeed, Confluent Education is characterized more by teacher-initiated activities and relies less on the total learning context or environment itself than the above discussed British Schools, Summerhill, and probably also the Danish Folk High Schools.

Modern Humanistic Education

A full and complete account of this very broad and varied movement is quite beyond the scope of this book, so I have selected only a few examples of this "genus," Modern Humanistic Education. I and many others have written specifically about Confluent Education, which I regard as a species/variant of the "genus," Humanistic Education. But I will not include a description or analysis of Confluent Education here because much of this book has been written to undertake that task. (See especially, the multivariate analyses in Chapter 1.)

I will include here (see Figure 2.1) the work of Weinstein and Fantini, Alschuler, and Simon, which comprised the main elements of the program in Humanistic Education of the University of Massachusetts at Amherst. I also include the work of Borton (1970) and Newberg (1977) as prototypes of Modern Humanistic Education—in addition to the Amherst group. Combs, originally a student of Carl Rogers, has also been very prolific in this field (Combs, 1962, 1971, 1975, 1982, 1988, 1991).

In a Ford Foundation Report, *Toward Humanistic Education, A Curriculum of Affect*, Weinsten and Fantini (1970) fulfilled the primary goal of the Ford-Esalen Project. This was to develop affective techniques that would enhance the existing curricula of the public schools in order to facilitate cognitive learning.

Weinstein and Fantini, however, approached this task in what I think was a "revolutionary" way. It was an approach to Humanistic Education which aimed for the development of a whole new curricular emphasis for the schools. This was called by them the "curriculum of concerns," in which the subject matter is the learner, his/her emotions, feelings, and thoughts in order to help develop a sense of identity, power, and connectedness to others. Thus, the affective domain became a subject, in the same way that mathematics, social studies, and English are subjects.

The other major approach to Humanistic Education was epitomized by Confluent Education, in which affect was infused with the cognitive content of the curriculum. The curriculum of concerns does not advocate or imply that academic subjects are not meaningful but, like Confluent Education, assumes that affective processes are a necessary part of the learning experience.

According to Lyon (1971, p. 75), ". . . Brown, Weinstein and their associates are *coordinating this important venture very closely* (this author's emphasis), and the Ford Foundation saw fit to financially support continued work for both of these *naturally complementary activities* (this author's emphasis)."

Thus, from the very beginning of these ventures, they were closely identified with one another and, indeed, were in the same Ford Foundation program on Affective Education—which was clearly understood as an approach to Humanistic Education. As noted in Chapter 3 (Critique, pp. 87-88), it was only later, in the mid to late 1970s, that Confluent Education separated itself from other similar programs in the Humanistic Education genre.

The evaluations of programs like this were not very thorough, as Lyon (1971, p. 288) stated: "At the present time Humanistic Education is a movement, rather than a discipline. It lacks a sound theoretical base and there is little research to prove, disprove, or improve the efficacy of its technique." And it is my contention, stated in Chapter 3 (Critique, p. 66), that these difficulties remained with most, if not all, the programs under the broad umbrella of Humanistic Education, with the possible exceptions of Newberg's Affective Education, and Alschuler's work on achievement motivation.

Norman Newberg was a consultant in curriculum development and teacher training in various school systems and universities in the United States, Canada, Israel, and Belgium. I have chosen the work outlined in his book *Affective Education in Philadelphia* (1977) as also representative of an approach to Humanistic Education. Note, however, that the title, including "Affective Education" marks it with the same original label as both Confluent Education and the University of Massachusetts group. It is important historically to see how the label of "Affective Education," not "Humanistic Education," was the common denominator of these three related, yet increasingly differentiated, programs over time.

There were three major aspects of Newberg's "Affective Education" program: (a) The Communications Network, which focused on improving listening, speaking, reading, and writing; (b) the Teacher Expectation Project, which is intended to raise teachers' awareness of how low expectations influence their students' abilities to learn; and (c) the Schools for All Ages, which stressed age-integration and independent and cooperative learning styles.

In Philadelphia, their work has focused on disadvantaged populations (like the early work of Weinstein and Fantini, 1968), but their curricula and methods also were apparently widely used in middle- and upper-income communities. In addition, according to Newberg (1977, p. 30), "Together with other colleagues in the field, we have been creating 'new mores' for schools, mores which give children more control over their lives, a greater respect and concern for others, and the pleasure of being successful learners."

Newberg (1977) claims that his methods do yield statistically significant improvements for students on reading, more persistence on tasks, and improve writing more than other students not in their affective classes. He also reports more positive attitudes about school, better attendance records, and less disciplinary actions. None of the data or details of these claims, however, are reported or cited in the literature.

Alfred Alschuler, another key member of the University of Massachusetts Center for Humanistic Education, had a somewhat different approach than the above-mentioned scholar/practitioners. He suggested for a typology for educational methods: *Congruent*, *Confluent*, and *Contextual* approaches (Simpson, 1976).

The Congruent approach was called "self-science." It focused on personal knowledge. Confluence adapts the cognitive-subject matter to include affective learning. Contextual training (e.g., Alschuler et al., 1977) involves organizational development to improve the climate of the school, including the relationship between teachers and students and coping with the system within which Humanistic Education occurs.

Alschuler (1970, 1973) also concentrated on developing achievement motivation in children, following the work of his mentor, David McClelland (1961) at Harvard. This emphasis and Alschuler's later work on values were central parts of what was called "*Psychological*

Education."

Perhaps more than anyone else in the University of Massachusetts Center for Humanistic Education, Sidney G. Simon (Raths, Harmin, & Simon, 1966; Simon, Howe, & Kirschenbaum, 1972; Read & Simon, 1975) along with his colleagues outside of that Center, Louis E. Raths, Donald A. Read, Merrill Harmin, and Howard Kirschenbaum, developed a strategy known as Values Clarification. Miller (1976) classifies Values Clarification as a "self-concept" orientation (as compared with Kohlberg's, 1971, moral development model, which he terms "developmental" or compared with human relations training in the National Training Laboratories (NTL), which he calls a "sensitivity and group orientation," and from Confluent Education, a "consciousness-expansion" approach).

In the Values Clarification model, Miller (p. 10) lists Simon, Raths, Harmin, and Kirschenbaum as the leading theorists and the incorporation of the valuing process as the major aim of the Values Clarification model.

The aim of the self-concept models, of which Values Clarification is one, is to help the student become aware of himself to the extent that he/she can guide his/her own behavior without excessive reference to others' expectations. This orientation, in which by 1976 Sidney Simon was probably the most prominent figure, centers on students' clarifying those values which are integral to self-concept development. This development is also assumed to develop identity, which is the centerpiece of much of Weinstein and Fantini's work in the curriculum of affect and in Alschuler's psychological education. In fact, Weinstein and Fantini have called their work "Identity Education" (Miller, 1976, p. 50).

There are many subprocesses in Values Clarification and for a complete account the reader is referred to Simon's and his colleagues' works and to Miller's (1976, p. 51) summary of these. Some of these include choosing freely from alternatives, after considering consequences, and consistently repeating these steps.

As mentioned above, the Values Clarification approach has many highly structured activities, situations, and questionnaires and are usually most appropriate for those teaching/counseling situations with students needing relatively high structure and an improved sense of personal identity in a warm and accepting atmosphere for sharing values.

According to Miller (1976, p. 55), "This has been a popular model with teachers. Because the approach is structured and easily applied to the classroom, teachers can quickly integrate it into their curriculum." While some teachers apparently have reported dramatic and encouraging changes in students with this method, I am unaware of careful scientific evaluations of its effects.

Finally, I think it is noteworthy that Miller (1976) regards such diverse educational methods as values clarification, moral development, psychosynthesis, synectics, psychological education, human relations training, meditation, and confluent education *all* as teaching approaches in *affective* education. Apparently Miller prefers "affective education" to "humanistic education" as a rubric to cover the genus, including a long and varied list of methods. This is important because others have regarded these two terms as practically synonymous (e.g., Brown, Weinstein and Fantini, Newberg). However, the confusion within the genre suggests a strong need for integration, to clarify the methods for teachers and theorists alike.

Miller (1976) seems to understand the need for clarification, definition, and integration of this diverse field (movement). In my opinion, he offers a helpful framework for affective teaching models, including diverse specific methods, with their leading theorists, their major orientation (e.g., developmental, self-concept, consciousness expansion, etc.), and their aims. But the definitional problem, so often referred to in this book, still remains, as evidenced by the historic and current efforts to provide a paradigmatic base for the field. It is as though we are still groping for that vital center or Confluent Gestalt, as I have mentioned in Chapter 3 on Critique (pp. 96-100).

For example, I'm not sure that Fairfield, Kurtz, and their secular humanist colleagues (Fairfield, 1971) would have thought of Humanistic Education as largely affective. Nor do I think that Alschuler (1970, 1973) did or would now think of his work in developing achievement motivation as exclusively affective. The Confluent Education group at Santa Barbara stressed a model which allegedly *combines* (this author's emphasis) affect and cognition and later the psychomotor domain (J. H. Brown, 1996). This integrative feature, I believe, was considered so essential that it was given as one of the reasons Confluent educators gradually separated themselves from the larger Humanistic Movement. Simpson (1976, p. viii) sees the "self-as-curriculum" as the common denominator in all these methods not limited to "education of affect." And, finally, Jarrett (1973), like Simpson, in his broad conception of the traditional humanities as a precursor to experiential, affective Humanistic Education, suggested (p. 105) that many educators of that day in the "cause" of Humanistic Education have *very different interests* (this author's emphasis) than academics advocating the humanities as a necessary study for developing "wholeness" and "humaneness" in society.

Another representative of Modern Humanistic Education in Figure 2.1 is Terry Borton. In my view, the following quote, from the preface of his book *Reach, Touch, and Teach* (1970), portrays him as squarely in the domain of identity education to improve the self-concept (see Patterson, 1973, p. 165 and Miller, 1976, p. 91). He was associated with the Center for Humanistic Education at Amherst and worked closely with Norman Newberg in Philadelphia. At the time of this book's publication, he was a Research Associate at Harvard University.

This book describes my attempt to *reach* students at basic personality levels, *touch* them as individual human beings, and yet *teach* them in an organized fashion.

I believe that what a student learns in school, and what he eventually becomes are significantly influenced by how he feels about himself and the world outside. I think that schools should legitimize these feelings, and should teach students a variety of ways to recognize and express them. An education without this understanding of self is simply training in an irrelevant accumulation of facts and theories—irrelevant because it is not related to what students *feel* is important. The goal of the teacher should be to help each student constantly increase his understanding of his feelings, and expand that self-awareness by utilizing the vast intellectual resources available to man. Such an education will mean that a student learns increasingly sophisticated *processes* for coping with his *concerns* about his inner self, and the outer world. By stressing the relation between processes and concerns, it should be possible to make school as relevant, involving, and joyful as the learning each of us experienced when we were infants first discovering ourselves and our surroundings. (Borton, 1970, p. vii)

This quote, it seems to me, places Borton in the center of the Affective Education Movement (this author's emphasis).

Critique of Borton's (1970) book comes from Robert E. Samples

(1970), who highlights the common flaw found in all the affective approaches, namely that the instructional strategies are not based on any systematic theory of human behavior and especially human development.

Arthur Combs, to whom I've referred earlier, was noted for his many contributions to the literature of Modern Humanistic Education. His focus was on perception, concepts, goals, teacher training, and schools, all more or less based on the groundwork of his mentor, Carl R. Rogers and Rogers' student-centered approach to education.

In summary, the instructional values of people in the Affective Education Movement are nearly identical with those values which I have analyzed and described in my OTL studies (Shapiro, 1985a, 1985b, 1986, 1987) and are found in detail in Chapter 1 of this book.

Patterson (1973), though identifying himself a "humanistic educator," as indicated in the title of his book and in his major argument (p. 189) that the major function of the schools is to produce self-actualizing persons (like the doctrine of Aristotle), has some critical comments to make on Affective Education approaches (see Miller, 1976, p. 15).

Patterson and many others (see Chapter 3 on Critique) feel there has been an overemphasis on techniques, and highly structured, teacher-initiated, teacher-controlled procedures. This, to him, is a major flaw in the purely affective approach of the workers in Modern Humanistic Education, whom I have selected as representative of the field. The possible exceptions to this are Alschuler, in his work on achievement motivation, and possibly some of Simon's work in Values Clarification.

Being too teacher-centered and not being soundly based on systematic theory appear to be some of the recurrent themes of criticism. In addition, Chapter 3 recounts the lack of solid empirical evaluation of the methods. The work of Alfred Alschuler, with David C. McClelland, appears to be a major exception to this widespread criticism. Affective or Humanistic Education has had many advocates over the years, especially when it has been based on identifiable theories of interpersonal relations, such as those of Rogers (1961, 1983) and Combs (1962, 1971, 1982, 1988).

The American Psychology of Personality, Humanistic Psychology, Gestalt Therapy, and the Group Dynamics Movement

Out of the rich mixture of concepts, methods, and philosophies of Phenomenology, Existentialism, and Humanism, the American Psychology of Personality emerged (Misiak & Sexton, 1973, p. 107). The most prominent American psychologists at this time was William James (1902/1985, 1923), often acknowledged as the father of American psychology, followed by Gordon Allport (1937, 1955, 1968), Gardner Murphy (1949), and Henry Murray (1938). Allport and Murray were colleagues at Harvard and students of James.

Nearly all of the originators of Phenomenology and Existentialism were European with the exception of William James, who influenced many philosophers and psychologists in Europe and America. Like the above mentioned American psychologists of personality, Humanistic Psychology was almost entirely American. The primary originators/founders of Humanistic Psychology, in my view, were Maslow (1943, 1950, 1968, 1970); Rogers (1961, 1969, 1983, 1985); May (1958, 1967, 1969a, 1969b, 1972, 1981); and Perls (1947, 1973). James F. T. Bugental (1963, 1978), Charlotte Bühler (1959, 1967), Anthony Sutich and Miles Vich (1962, 1969) were prominent among its implementors in its early stages. I also regard Perls in this category, in addition to his special contribution of Gestalt Therapy (see Figure 2.1).

Some of the major contributors to Humanistic Education were G. I. Brown (1971, 1975); Richard Jones (1968); Gerald Weinstein and Mario Fantini (1970); Alfred Alschuler (1969, 1973); Sidney Simon (1972); Norman Newberg (1977); Arthur Combs (1962); Carl Rogers (1969, 1985); and Terry Borton (1970).

Among the many early and prominent appliers (outside of K-12 education) were Lee Bradford, Jack Gibb, and Kenneth Benne (1964) from the field of group dynamics; Robert Tannenbaum (Tannenbaum & Schmidt, 1958; Tannenbaum, Weschler, & Massarik, 1961); and Chris Argyris (1962, 1964, 1971, 1976) to management, higher education, and a wide variety of organizations and institutions. Uri Merry and George I. Brown (1987), James Barott and Justein Klieveland (1996), as well as myself were later appliers of Humanistic Psychology to organizational development, and to schools.

While there is no question that the Gestalt Therapy of Frederick S.

("Fritz") Perls was and is very influential in Confluent Education, tracing Gestalt Therapy to its alleged major precursor, Gestalt Psychology is *much more* tenuous. (See discussion on pp. 89-90 in Chapter 3, Critique.)   According to some scholars in Gestalt Psychology, Henle (1977), Arnheim (1974), and Popplestone and McPherson (1988, p. 150), "Gestalt Therapy was primarily Perls' invention in that he did not apply most of the major principles and misapplied others." In addition, according to Coleman (1994, p. 1185), "Gestalt approaches have not been subject to any amount of empirical research, which is in part a consequence of the ethos of the movement and the lack of precision in specifying models and methods." This lack of specification, to me, further suggests a tenuous relationship between Gestalt Psychology and Gestalt Therapy. However, other writers (H. Graham, 1986; J. R. Brown, 1996; Barott & Klieveland, 1996) see a much more direct relationship between the principles of Gestalt Psychology and the Gestalt Therapy developed by Perls.

Whatever its sources, the character analysis of Wilhelm Reich (1949), Zen Buddhism per Suzuki (1965), Tao according to Lao Tsu (1972),[5] the organismic theories of Kurt Goldstein (1939, 1940), Jacob Moreno's Psychodrama (1946) or European Existentialism, Gestalt Therapy has had a profound and lasting effect on both the teaching/training methodology and the research in Confluent Education to this day (1998). This condition was directly attributable to George and Judith Brown.   George Brown was not only the head of the academic program at UCSB for many years, he was also the Chief Investigator for three Ford Foundation Grants.

Like several other approaches in the genre of Humanistic Education (e.g., Self-Science, Student-Centered Schools, The Curriculum of Affect, and Values Clarification), Confluent Education became a major variant in programs which applied Humanistic Psychology to

---

[5]Perls was said to have been influenced by Eastern Religion in developing his personal identity and in his work in Gestalt Therapy (especially Taoism and Zen Buddhism; see Smith (Ed.), 1976, pp. 4, 33, 359). However, in Figure 2.1 (this chapter), I did *not* include Eastern Religion on the flow chart because whatever religious influence there was via Perls was indirect and not easily detectable (by me) in classrooms, seminars, nor in the assigned readings in the Confluent Education Program.   To my knowledge, Taoism and Zen were seldom, if ever, discussed in the Confluent Education Program.   It was strictly secular, and I am not aware that the "Meta" position, for example, was explicitly linked to Buddhism.

education. This connection of the Human Potential Movement, Humanistic Education, and Humanistic Psychology, including the Encounter Group Movement, to the specifically Confluent approach to teaching and learning was originally identified as one of the affective modes of education and as psychological education (see Brown, 1971, p. 3).

In addition to George Brown, the Esalen-trained group of teachers in the Santa Barbara area were instrumental in its development (see Hillman, 1973; Brown, 1971, 1975; and Yoemans, 1975a, 1975b). Prominent members of this group of experienced teachers included Aaron Hillman, Robin Montz, Gloria Castillo, Thomas Yoemans, and the late Beverly Galyean from the Los Angeles City Schools. The late Nils M. Grenstadt from Norway was also an early leader and expedited the Confluent approach in Norway, along with George and Judith Brown.

As noted previously, the work of the first two Ford Grants is reported in 1971 in *Human Teaching for Human Learning: An Introduction to Confluent Education.* This was the first book published on Confluent Education and is, therefore, a landmark work in the history of Confluent Education.

The greatly expanded second Ford Foundation Grant for over $350,000 was not specifically Esalen-based and included at least 50 teachers and consultants and was not limited to K-12. It included community colleges and universities and was known as the DRICE grant (Development and Research in Confluent Education) and was reported on in 1975 with the second seminal book, *The Live Classroom* (1975) also edited by G. I. Brown, T. Yoemans, and L. Grizzard.

Returning to the flow chart in Figure 2.1, on the right hand side from the philosophy of Humanism has come "early" Humanistic Education, previously mentioned and the traditional disciplines of the Humanities, such as liberal arts, philosophy, literature, history, and languages. The latter purposely ends without a connection to the flow to early Humanistic and Progressive Education Movements which deeply influenced Modern Humanistic Education. The latter, along with the U.S. Mental Health Movement mentioned by Simpson (1976, pp. 11-14), which flowed through Modern Humanistic Education to the Human Potential Movement, in my view, did contribute to the development of Confluent Education.

The Group Dynamics Movement initiated by the National Training

Laboratory at Bethel, Maine, which originated in 1946, also became a significant force in Confluent Education (Shapiro & Mortola, 1996, pp. 81-94). Both the Mental Health Movement and Group Dynamics did have direct influence on Confluent Education but were not major contributions. Tracing their sources is considered outside the scope of this chapter. Note that they both are framed by ovals, rather than rectangles, and show no antecedents on Figure 2.1. This does not mean that the field of Group Dynamics is not related to Humanistic Psychology/Education, but I see these relationships as complex and largely indirect. An exception was the work of Kurt Lewin (1936), who earlier could be seen as part of Gestalt (Field Theory) Psychology, as well as one of the founders of Group Dynamics.

The three major precursors of Confluent Education, as I understand it, were Humanistic Psychology, Humanistic Education, and Gestalt Therapy. All three held the central values of the *expression of affect*, emphasis on the *whole person as an individual* with intrinsic dignity and worth, *self-actualization through personal growth* and *bonding with other individuals*. Much of this bonding took place in small encounter groups in growth centers like Esalen in California and Findhorn in Scotland, and the Meta-senter in Norway.

In addition to affect (expressive individualism), connectedness, and personal growth, the other most basic value, in my opinion, was *process-orientation* in encounter-like growth groups, and in the various psychological and body therapies, as well as part of lifestyle. Content and future goals were subordinated to being fully-present in "the eternal now." This process-orientation involved deep and continuous exchange of current emotions and feelings and perceptions *ideally* (this author's emphasis) in a nonjudgmental, authentic way. Thus, the rejection of dwelling on the past or speculating (often called "fantasy") about the future were regarded as losing contact with the alleged *only* (this author's emphasis) available reality ("the what and how of the here and now").

Unfortunately, when carried to extremes, I think this degree of present-centeredness reduces the context of the subcultures of growth groups, Gestalt Therapy, etc. and, therefore, the previous characterization of Confluent Education (in Academia) as a high-context culture becomes more problematic. Individualism as a philosophy and guide for behavior was previously cited as a value more characteristic of low-context cultures like modern USA and Germany, for example.

However, I suspect that this "problem" of decontextualization was seldom, if ever, recognized as such, and became of much greater concerns to academics, like myself, than the enthusiastic participants in the later 1960s and mid-1970s in the widespread Human Potential Movement, especially in this country.

To recapitulate Figure 2.1, in my opinion, the methods and values of Gestalt Therapy, Humanistic Psychology, and Modern Humanistic Education, mentioned earlier (indicated by heavy lines on the diagram) were the three most potent immediate forces in the origins of Confluent Education (1966), during the first Ford Foundation Grant at Esalen.

The history of Confluent Education as an academic program at UCSB has been discussed extensively in Chapter 1.

Humanistic Psychology

From the many sources on Humanistic Psychology (e.g., *Humanistic Psychology: New Frontiers*, edited by Nevill, 1977; *Humanistic Psychology: Concepts and Criticisms*, edited by Royce & Mos, 1981; *The Human Face of Psychology*, Graham, 1986; "The Humanistic Movement in Psychology: History, Celebration and Prospects," *The Humanistic Psychologist*, 20(2 & 3), 1992; Bugental, 1964; Bühler, 1967; and Bühler & Allen, 1967), I have selected *Humanistic Psychology: A Synthesis* (Tageson, 1982) to represent this genre.

My selection of Tageson's (1982) work to epitomize Modern Humanistic Psychology greatly simplifies the exposition of this broad and diverse field. But two other basic reasons for doing this are that Tageson provides a clear and much needed synthesis of this field and, at the same time, considers the wide intellectual territory of the history and various practices of this widespread and varied movement.

In checking through his bibliography and index, I found that Tageson (1982) includes references to every single box or oval in Figure 2.1, my map of the Origins of Confluent Education. To me, the least obvious connections of Tageson's references are to the "Traditional Humanities." These references are scattered and somewhat indirect. But, nevertheless, in my opinion, they are there.

Philosophy and Literature appear to be the two broad disciplines with the most references by Tageson. Examples are Nuttin's (1962) philosophy of self-realization, derived directly from Aristotle's

Teleology (Tageson, 1982, p. 16). Issues such as personal liberty; the literature of freedom and dignity are covered. Selected works of Aristotle, Plato, and Socrates; Frankl's (1947) studies on meaning; and Sartre's version of Existentialism are also included.

Literary references include Skinner's novel, *Walden Two*; Sartre's novels; Dunne's (1973) *Time and Myth*; and Perry's (1976) *Roots of Renewal in Myth and Madness*. There are also references to mythology, archetypes, and language, the latter exemplified by Chomsky's (1972) work on *Language and Mind*. Biography is also included, originally suggested by Allport (1942) and later by Bugental (1965) and Bühler (1965).

Thus, some of the traditional humanities are ways of knowing that are instrumentally utilized by these diverse scholars to understand issues of Tageson's (1982) central concern, Humanistic Psychology. These "humanities" references are not being included here for their own sake or for "enlarging the human spirit" or "increasing valuative responsiveness" in the scholars, readers, or students of the humanities in the usual disciplinary or academic sense.

Returning to Figure 2.1, The Flow Chart of the Origins of Confluent Education, I counted in Tageson (1982) 38 direct references to representatives of the various fields or movements. Sometimes the movements were cited as "The Human Potential Movement" (pp. 194, 228-230) and "Psychoanalysis" (pp. 8-9, 11, 19, 41), and "Humanistic Medicine" (pp. 239-241) as part of the Post-World War II Mental Health Movement.

It was very revealing to me that Tageson's (1982) work covered so many of the important precursors of Confluent Education and, as mentioned above, his synthesis (major themes) of Humanistic Psychology were also very helpful. Briefly, these are: The *Phenomenological Approach*; *Holism* (especially Lewin's, 1952, and Goldstein's, 1940, work); the *Actualizing Tendency*, including trusting the organism and the role of consciousness; *Self-Determination* (the developmental view); the *Ideal of Authenticity*; *Self-Transcendence*, including the transpersonal level; and, finally, *Person-Centeredness*, probably the most central theme of all, in my opinion.

I also became aware of the similarity of the Orientation to Learning (OTL) variables and factors I described in my multivariate and ordinary language analyses of Humanistic Education to his themes of Humanistic Psychology. This includes both the Transpersonal variable and the Transpersonal factor I found in the literature on Humanistic Education and which added to my original work on the OTL. George Leonard's book, *Education and Ecstasy* (1968), Thomas Robert's *Four Psychologies Applied to Education* (1975), and even in the later work of Carl Rogers were examples of the breakthrough from *secular* Humanistic Psychology and Education to the spiritual realm. These investigations led to development of the Transpersonal Orientation to Learning (TOTL) by myself and Louise Fitzgerald in 1989.

However, as Iannaccone has stated (in J. H. Brown, Ed., *Advances in Confluent Education*, 1996, p. 173), the spiritual/transpersonal level was seldom acknowledged in the entirely secular approach of Confluent Education. The only possible exception to this was the work of Thomas Yoemans in Psychosynthesis but, in my view, this was *never* mainstream indoctrination in Confluent Education in the 30 years I have known it.

The Human Potential Movement (1962-1990)

Reference to Figure 2.1 indicates that the three major influences in the origins of Confluent Education were filtered through the "Human Potential Movement," which requires some explanation in order to more completely understand the origins of Confluent Education.

As I understand it, the Human Potential Movement with all its diverse theories and techniques became very much a part of the American and Western European Zeitgeist from the late 1960s to the middle or late 1970s. And again referring to Tageson (1982, pp. 228-230) and Anderson (1983, pp. 64-72), the embodiment of this broad movement was the growth center, epitomized by Esalen in California and, perhaps, by Findhorn in Scotland.

For a period of time there were many such personal growth centers. Mann (1979) explains that growth centers are designed to provide an organizational setting for diverse approaches, ranging from encounter groups, support groups, body work, hatha yoga, massage to Zen meditation classes, sensory awareness and movement techniques, dance, bioenergetics, etc.

Many leaders were not necessarily licensed or professionally certified in psychiatry, psychology, counseling, or even massage. The major emphasis was on experiential consciousness-raising. The clients were self-selected and usually "seekers" for new styles of life and personal growth. Most were *not* specifically seeking psychotherapy per se.

There were several criticisms of the Human Potential Movement, particularly in the form of personal growth centers. First, there was the lack of formal qualifications of some of the workshop leaders and the lack of any serious selection process for the seminars, workshops, and various procedures aside from self-selection. Also there was a *notorious* (this author's emphasis) lack of outcome evaluation (e.g., of any particular program and of the general developmental process from encounter groups to Perls-led Gestalt groups to body awareness and, finally, to mystical or transpersonal/spiritually oriented practices).

Through the 1980s and 1990s, both the sheer number of growth centers and the impact of the Human Potential Movement itself sharply declined and fractionated into entrepreneurial movements like EST or Guru-led enclaves like that of Rajneesh. Furthermore, the political implications of the Human Potential Movement came to be seriously out of step with mainstream conservative values which surged in the 1980s and partially continue in the 1990s.

While it was also true that Confluent Education and the Curriculum of Affect were first nurtured as Ford-Esalen projects in Affective Education, their connections with the Human Potential Movement and Personal Growth Centers also became significantly attenuated in the 1980s and 1990s. Nevertheless, it is noteworthy that the original *name*, as well as the Gestalt approach itself, were originated *at Esalen* (this author's emphasis) as "Confluent Education." So its heritage from the Human Potential Movement and centers like Esalen is very significant, in my view. (See Chapter 1 for more specific references.)

The "Human Potential Movement" label originated from Aldous Huxley (1954) who had spoken of "human potentialities" (p. 69). First, a series of programs at Esalen were offered under the heading "The Human Potentiality" in the summer of 1962 by its founders, Michael Murphy and Richard Price.

Originally, in its era of lofty thoughts and intellectual discourse, it was known by Murphy and Price as Esalen's "Apollonian" age, in which its common project was the "Vision." This was a vision of what could be made to happen: a major cultural change, an evolutionary leap. But this "Vision" was elusive and needed concreteness, a core of ideas and also to be made respectable academically and professionally (Anderson, 1983, p. 65).

In addition to Aldous Huxley and his wife Laura, Abraham Maslow made a vital contribution to the Vision by contrasting his studies of healthy, fully functioning, self-actualizing people (Maslow, 1968, *Toward a Psychology of Being*) with the pathological emphasis of Freudian and the mechanics of behavioral psychology. Maslow also connected his work with the earlier work of William James (1902/1985), *Varieties of Religious Experience*) and was especially active during the Apollonian period of Esalen.

Even in the intellectual period of Esalen's development, the work of serious psychological/philosophical inquiries in the recommended readings were supplemented with evolutionary theory, Eastern and Western religions (e.g., esoteric doctrines of Buddhist and Hindu philosophy), and especially intuitive thinking to balance rational positivism with literature from religion, art, and nature.

This so-called Apollonian period was, however, short-lived because, almost from the beginning, there was an "expressed yearning for something else, some way of turning those lofty concepts into lived reality" (Anderson, 1983, p. 69). The criticisms of rationality grew, especially by such luminaries as Willis Harman, Alan Watts, and Gregory Bateson. They were expressing some of the more explosive ideas of the mid-20th century, for example, that Western social belief systems of that time and definitions of reality itself were only *relative truths* (this author's emphasis) open to challenge and subject to change.

Esalen seminars on LSD, in late 1962, approximately one year before it was discovered by the national media, began to appear and promoted its use and the psychedelic movement per se. This was the beginning of the end of the intellectualized nature of the activities at Esalen led by Aldous Huxley (1954).

Timothy Leary and Richard Alpert, both young psychologists at Harvard's Center for Research in Personality, were discharged by Harvard for their research on psychedelics and joined together, proclaiming that a psychedelic, psychological revolution was about to take place and that the use of these drugs would result in transcendent religious experience *within reach of everyone* (this author's emphasis). Shortly after their dismissal from Harvard, Alan Watts joined Leary and Alpert. Watts had become a central figure at Esalen and very much identified with the Human Potential Movement. Michael Murphy himself had already had his own experience with hallucinogenic drugs, just before the first seminar series on Human Potentialities and, thereby, the stage was set to move Esalen away from an intellectually-oriented center. It had been largely led by professors of psychology and philosophy from Stanford University, from which Murphy had graduated as a psychology major.

The second Human Potentiality series at Esalen in the winter and spring of 1963 started "a distinct shift toward more variety" (Anderson, 1983, p. 79) and the full blooming of the Human Potential Movement followed rapidly into its "Dionysian" phase. These new developments of encounter groups, Gestalt Therapy, and body work became the mainstays of the Esalen programs.

It is noteworthy that encounter groups and Gestalt Therapy also became central to the curriculum of Confluent Education, but body work (e.g., massage, Rolfing, body movement, Feldenkreis, etc.) received almost no emphasis in the Confluent agenda. The main reason for this, in my view, is that the major professors were not schooled in these body-oriented techniques *and* (this author's emphasis) that their risk to academic respectability were judged to be considerably greater than encounter and Gestalt, which already were regarded as anti-intellectual and, therefore, questionable by the academics and administrators at UCSB.

From encounter or sensitivity groups, Gestalt Therapy, and body work, the three principle components of Esalen's programming, there grew the incredible Dionysian variety of programs which characterized the Human Potential Movement. Its very breadth and prominence justify considering it a social movement, much more so than Gestalt Therapy or even widely varying body approaches and the Eastern/mystical approaches which also abounded at Esalen. The latter occurred in many loci outside of Esalen and were not transferred to Confluent Education—for essentially the same reasons sensory awareness and body work per se were not a part of the Confluent curriculum. As mentioned above, Psychosynthesis, with its "higher Self" and mystical overtones, were also minimized in the Confluent Program at UCSB, although there were a few transpersonally oriented students and leaders in the program (especially Thomas Yoemans).

Given the above narrative about Esalen and the Human Potential Movement, reference to Figure 2.1 indicates that the three largest contributors to the origins of Confluent Education (Gestalt Therapy, Modern Humanistic Psychology, and Modern Humanistic Education) were all filtered through the Human Potential Movement. This represented the Zeitgeist of that time (i.e., the middle 1960s to the late 1970s).

The Group Dynamics Movement did have considerable influence on the Human Potential Movement and also had an identifiable connection and influence largely due to my own role as an NTL-trained major professor in the Confluent Program from 1970 to 1991. This continued after my retirement in 1990 (see J. H. Brown, 1996, chap. 6, pp. 81-94).

The Post-World War II Mental Health Movement also directly contributed to Confluent Education according to Figure 2.1 and it probably bordered on the Human Potential Movement via various psychiatrists, psychologists, and psychiatric social workers. Many of these professionals were sympathetic to the Human Potential Movement. However, a significant number of them remained distant and negatively disposed toward Humanistic Psychology, which after all, like the Human Potential Movement, rejected psychoanalysis, electric-shock treatment, mental hospitals, and pharmaceutical interventions for the mentally disturbed. Further, many of the Mental Health professionals were pathology-oriented and retained the medical model which, to some extent, also shaped depth psychologies like Psychoanalysis and Jungian analysis as interventions for the so-called "neurotic personalities of our time" (see Karen Horney, 1937 and Fritz Perls, 1969).

Conclusions

First, I am struck by what I perceive to be the "embeddedness" of Confluent Education in the many philosophies and methodologies depicted in Figure 2.1. Apparently, Confluent Education has many progenitors, some remote, some recent, and many still active.

Secondly, I sense a kind of recurring historical "*Humanist Impulse*" in the various cultures and disciplines which this review has encompassed. This phenomenon will be discussed further in the final Summary and Interpretation.

Third, the origins of Confluent Education depicted in Figure 2.1, to me, suggest a recontextualization of identification and placement in time. To see Confluent Education as embedded in the Human Potential Movement and to understand the spirit of that movement widens my perspective and deepens my appreciation of Confluent Education.

Finally, having something of an overview might provide much-needed perspective on the fate of other innovative programs and movements. For example, it has been most revealing to me that the more remote the ancestor, the more I *underestimated* (this author's emphasis) the vagueness, diversity, and inner contradictions of most of these progenitors. Some of these features might be prominent in our genes. This, however, does not diminish the point that such an umbrella like-heritage requires *more*, not less careful analysis and reflection.

Chapter 3

A Critique of Confluent Education

In my view, a sustained, coherent critique of Confluent Education, with a few partial exceptions, is nowhere to be found. There are several recent scattered examples of serious critiques like those of Hackbarth (1996, pp. 18-19), George Brown (1996, pp. ix-xiv), and Moheno (1996, pp. 21-22). The most sustained critiques in my view come from Iannaccone (1996, pp. 171-174) and Brown's earlier piece in 1975 (pp. 295-300).

Iannaccone points out the definitional problem, the lack of a core concept, and especially, the missing "confluence" of affect, cognitions, and action. He further cites a "missing dimension," that of spirituality. Nevertheless, his discussion is quite limited in its details.

Brown (1975) himself provides the most sustained source of what might be considered the vulnerability of Confluent theory and methods to misuse or damage. For example, as discussed later in this chapter, he claims that "healthy skepticism" about the theory that growth and development of *all* human potential is good and considers cases where it might be counterproductive. For example, much of mankind does not really desire these changes and a counterreaction could be created if the growth is too rapidly accelerated. He also had some caveats regarding the application of Confluent techniques as teacher "gimmicks" (as did Bogad, 1975, p. 159), and that Confluent Education being "value-free" can be misused or downright destructive. Finally, Brown warns us against unawareness of how Confluent approaches might meet the inner needs of the purveyors without regard to its effects on students or clients.

However, Brown cites the seemingly foolproof safeguards of feedback and awareness training, and the completely voluntary nature of student participation in the *affective* experiences. He also adds the observation that he and his group know of *no* students who have been harmed by their work.

While I find these caveats useful, there are no comprehensive accounts of serious follow up and openness to remedial evaluation and no *balanced* (this author's emphasis) reviews of the effects of Confluent Education (especially long term effects on learning). Sources for the task of a critique are widely distributed, as the following list demonstrates:

1.   Three recent (1996) books which are serious attempts to portray the current Confluent approach, representing many authors. These are:

(a) *Advances in Confluent Education: Integrating Consciousness for Human Change*, Joel H. Brown, Editor. This is a survey of the current work of 14 authors.

(b) *Educating Our 21st Century Adventurers* by Phillip B. B. Moheno is a slightly expanded and updated report of his doctoral dissertation (Moheno, 1985). This book describes the empirical development and implications of his instrument to measure Confluent classroom behavior of secondary math and science student teachers. His instrument the "Humanistic/Confluent Interactional Analysis Category System (HCIACS)" was derived from microanalysis of videotapes of classroom interactions between teachers and students. Although he extended this work toward postulating a basic paradigm for Confluent Education, he did not include my own multivariate research as a stepping stone toward his own paradigmatic statements.

(c) *The I in Science: Training to Utilize Subjectivity in Research* by Judith R. Brown. This book is a description of a course given at the University of Oslo, Norway over a 4-year period. It also includes a formulation and implications of a totally *subjective* (this author's emphasis) approach only to *qualitative* (this author's emphasis) research in *social* science.

These three current (1996) books taken together, in my view, represent the broadest and most recent expression of Confluent theory and practice since the 1975 publication of *The Live Classroom*, edited by G. I. Brown, T. Yoemans, and L. Grizzard, and the much briefer mini-book in 1976, *Getting It All Together: Confluent Education* by G. I. Brown, M. Phillips, and myself. So these most recent works fill a 20-year gap. *The Neurotic Behavior of Organizations* (Merry & Brown, 1987) was published in this alleged gap but was a theoretical, specialized application of Confluent Education to organizations and I do not consider it to be in the same genre as the original nor very recent books. With the exception of Judith Brown's book, there are widely dispersed portions of significant critique in these books.

2. Four studies conducted by myself, which include both strengths and weakness of Confluent Education follow:

(a) An in-depth interview survey (1995) of 16 senior UCSB professors and administrators on "How Do You Understand What Happened to the Confluent Education Program Here at UCSB?"

(b) A recent (1995-96) interview survey of 40 mature graduates of the M..A. and Ph.D. Confluent Program on "The Best and Worst Features of Confluent Education."

(c) The results of an exercise in 1985 in a course on Issues in Confluent Education (ED 288b), in which "Strengths" and "Blocks" in the program were listed by the students.

(d) In 1986 there were many unsolicited, highly critical responses from local high school teachers when asked to take the OTL instrument. This questionnaire measures a Humanistic/Confluent orientation to instruction. These data are aggregated below.

3. Previously cited, *The Journal of Humanistic Psychology* article, pp. 80-105; S. B. Shapiro (1997), "The UCSB Confluent Education Program: Its Essence and Demise," widely disseminated evaluations of the whole Human Potential Movement, including Humanistic Psychology and Humanistic Education (e.g., previously cited Bellah et al., 1985; Friedman, 1992; Koch, 1971; Mosher & Sprinthall, 1971; Patterson, 1973; Plumb, 1993; Smith, 1991).

Before proceeding with the discussion of all these sources and an extensive critique, it may be well to state my understanding of the term/concept of "critique."

I understand the concept of critique as a *critical examination* (this author's emphasis) of a work, especially in comparison to certain explicit standards. It is often a commentary, analysis, evaluation, or review of the literature in question and *can* (this author's emphasis) include merits as well as faults. It is also considered an art or practice more than a science, but it usually needs to be systematic and thorough and have an explanatory purpose and possibly a remedial function. I would only add that in this case, it should be "fair" and *balanced* (this author's emphasis), covering both positive and negative aspects of Confluent Education, but perhaps *leaning to the critical side* (this author's emphasis). (Other sections of this book cover the many constructive features of the Confluent approach.) Critique also should be thorough in the scholarly sense, include representative coverage of the field, hopefully stimulate thoughtful discussion and possibly corrective action. Finally, in my opinion, it should avoid "ad hominem" criticism or praise and the author's opinion should be made clearly separate from views from other sources.

Having set forth the above explication of the rather demanding criteria for constructive critique, it comes as no surprise that it is largely missing in Confluent and other humanistic literature. But there is and has been an increasing quantity of material critical of the broader humanistic movement of which I think Confluent Education is a part. Much of this somewhat revisionist criticism of Humanistic Psychology, Humanistic Education, and other related fields is found in humanistically oriented literature, as well as from other sources "outside" the Human Potential Movement. (See additional "outside" sources: Back, 1972; Cox, 1973; Groothuis, 1986; Hirsch, 1987, 1996; Lasch, 1976; Lieberman, Yalom, & Miles, 1973; Marin, 1975, p. 46; Mintz, 1973, p. 42; Samples, 1970; Shur, 1976.)

Interviews of Senior Faculty and Administrators

In order to gain perspective on the Confluent Education Program at UCSB, in 1995 the author interviewed 16 current and past senior faculty members from the Department of Education. Many of the 16 professors have been administrators (4 Deans and 3 non-overlapping Chairpersons).

The basic question put to these interviewees was "How do you account for (explain/understand) what happened to the Confluent Education Program at UCSB?"

From the 16 subjects in the inquiry, 95 explanatory items were derived since each interviewee could report more than one explanation. Thus, there were nearly six identifiable responses per interview. Table 3.1 reports these perceptions.

Apparently a complex, interrelated set of factors which largely accounted for the *uniqueness* of the program were also significant in the perceived causes of its demise. Some of the *basic causes* for the demise of this unique program (e.g., perceived weak conceptual base, inability to replace retiring professors) can also be interpreted as *symptoms* of systemic defects. These defects have been perceived both

Table 3.1

Summary of "Causal Factors in the 'Fate' of Confluent Education at UCSB"

1.   (21 Responses)   **Perceived Weak Conceptual/Disciplinary Base.** (Therefore, definitional and identity problems persisted and still did in 1995 and the quality and quantity of research was regarded as "dubious" over the years.)

2.   (18 Responses)   **Senior Faculty Retired and Not Replaced.** (The program never regenerated itself academically, as shown by four successive unsuccessful searches to replace retiring faculty.) Apparently, the pool of suitable applicants was surprisingly (to me) limited. (Was this due to the alleged *uniqueness* of the program?)

3.   (16 Responses)   **Controversial Professors.** (Difficult personalities and uncompromising positions on issues of importance, poor communication with other professors and programs. Too dependent on *particular* professors whose personal needs too often superseded the alleged "confluent process" per se and its applications (e.g., "Gestalt-dominated").)

4.   (15 Responses)   **Non-Adaptive Responses to Change.** (The original vision, mission, and major purpose was lost (i.e., applications to classrooms) as the student body and community needs were changing (e.g., increasing needs for technology and cross-cultural teaching). It was seen as caught in a "time-warp" with essentially the same methods as in late 1960s and early 1970s.))

5.   (13 Responses)   **Active Opposition.**   There was continued opposition to the program within the department and across campus by both faculty and the administration. Support for the program weakened after the Ford Foundation Grants circa late 1970s and early 1980s. Most of the "opposition" perceived the program as contrary to the department's needs for status/academic respectability in a competitive academic culture.

6.   (12 Responses)   **Systemic Defects.** (There was the appearance of increasing isolation from other department programs and especially isolation from similar programs in other academic centers. The systemic function of corrective feedback to the program as a whole was never well developed. Constructive criticism was often treated as *attacks* on the professors and/or the program. It was as though the Confluent Program never really belonged in a School of Education. Finally, the Confluent Education Program became an embarrassment to a considerable number of influential people in the Graduate School of Education and others across campus.)

in the specific program at UCSB *and* in other humanistically oriented programs in education and psychology. Some of the most frequently mentioned shortcomings were: anti-intellectualism, over-emphasis on feelings, individualism, and not being responsive to rapidly changing social and political conditions.

In reviewing the above data (with some admitted speculation and reservations), it still appears to me that there were enough widely shared doubts and substantive criticisms of Confluent Education at UCSB, that when the crucial opportunity came (retirement of all of the senior professors apparently holding the program together), the program rapidly collapsed. It was easily *"merged out of existence"* as noted in the previous section on the history of the program at UCSB. "It was just a matter of time," one senior administrator said.

In summary, a triad of concerns, illustrated in Figure 3.1, were held accountable for what happened by this group of 16 senior professors and administrators.

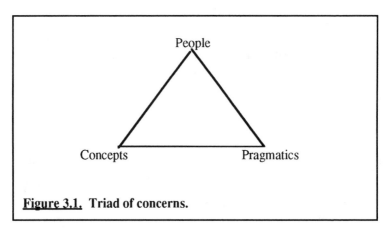

Figure 3.1. Triad of concerns.

These three basic concerns were distributed as Table 3.2 indicates.

The information in Table 3.2 indicates that *pragmatic issues* were determinant in policies and politics; for example, older faculty not being replaced as they retired, active opposition to the program from within the Department and across the campus. All these issues played an important role, and systemic defects like isolation from other and different programs in the Department of Education at UCSB also were

Table 3.2		
Summary of Concerns about Confluent Education by 16 Professors/Administrators of Education at UCSB		
Concern	Number of References	Percentage of References
Conceptual	36	37.9
Pragmatic	43	45.3
People	16	16.8
Total	95	100.0

prominent.

Conceptual issues mentioned included a weak conceptual research and knowledge base and this was considered by the interviewees a strong *second* reason for the demise of Confluent Education at UCSB. Conceptual issues were also perceived to be involved in the persistent identity and definitional problems which apparently existed from the very beginning of the program in 1966 until its very end in 1993.

Under *"People-related" issues*, there was a shared perception of "controversial" professors, but the "people-related" issues only accounted for about one sixth of the "weight" (emphases leading to the demise of the program). Included in this perception of the symptoms of being controversial were poor communication with other professors and programs, too much dependency on *particular* professors, and especially emphasis on their personal/individual needs and perspectives versus the needs of students in other programs in the Department. This also was considered to be detrimental to our own students' academic preparation and standards.

The Best-Worst Study

In the spring of 1996, I conducted brief interviews with 40 mature, local Confluent graduates (including both M.A.s and Ph.D.s) around the question, "What were the best and the worst features of Confluent Education as you experienced it?"

Table 3.3 indicates the responses representing the "Best" features of the program and Table 3.4 shows the summation of this data.

Note the powerful influence of "people-related" issues in Table 3.3. For example, the "Best" features of Confluent Education, the quality of the people and "people-related" issues, are almost 13 times as frequent as the conceptual concerns, and double the frequency of pragmatic concerns. These data contrast strongly to the perceived "Worst" features of Confluent Education, as shown in Table 3.5. The summation of this data is shown in Table 3.6.

Note in Table 3.5 that conceptual issues dominate the perceived "Worst" features of Confluent Education, accounting for over one half of the responses; whereas the criticism of the features of people represents only 13.7% of the weight given to all the "Worst" features. Does this data confirm the "affective bias" noted in Confluent Education as I indicated in the OTL studies (Shapiro, 1985, 1987) and others? To me these data suggest that even our own students were critical of the identity/definitional weakness and the lack of academic credibility. This included seemingly paradoxical/contradictory features of the program.

The perceived pragmatic deficiencies in the program again received moderate emphasis—less than the conceptual flaws and more than the people-related flaws, like the lack of student and professorial quality. In the pragmatic area of the basic triad, the usual criticisms appeared, related to a lack of practical knowledge and applicability, the unbalanced (affectively biased) nature of the curriculum, etc. Also, there was a perception of lack of any formal certification or apprenticeship opportunities.

When the "Best" and the "Worst" features derived from this study are combined, the following observations serve to summarize the results:

1.   The "Worst" has somewhat (about 55% to 45%) more items reported than the "Best" (73 to 59 totals, respectively).

2.   In the "Worst" category, *people* were only listed in 13.7% of the responses, but in the "Best" features they constituted 64.4% of the responses (almost five times as frequently as in the "Worst" features). So, while the quality of the people here is perceived *by far* as the best feature of Confluent Education, its worst features are significantly

Table 3.3

The "Best" Features of Confluent Education Perceived by 40 M.A. and Ph.D. Graduates of the Program

Frequency	Rank for Frequency	Best Features	Triad Classification
11	1	The *quality* of the people (professors and students), bonding, warmth, respect, trust	People
8	2.5	Expression and encouragement of *affect* and experiential learning	People
8	2.5	Opportunity for personal development	People
6	4.5	Relevance to the needs of individuals	Pragmatic
6	4.5	Quality of the professors as human beings	People
5	6.5	Applicability—Broadly and directly applicable to my work	Pragmatic
5	6.5	Professional development	Pragmatic
3	8.5	Integration of understanding feelings and concepts	Conceptual
3	8.5	Diversity of students—ethnic, nationality, gender, cultural	People
2	10.5	Authenticity of the people involved	People
2	10.5	Flexibility of the program	Pragmatic
Total 59			

Table 3.4

<u>**Summation of Data on "Best" Features of Confluent Education**</u>

Concern	Number of References	Percentage of References
Conceptual	3	5.1
Pragmatic	18	30.5
People	38	64.4
Total	59	100.0

conceptual and have relatively little to do with people issues.

3.   In the "Worst" feature count, conceptual problems were more than one half the responses, but in the "Best" category, conceptual issues were only mentioned about 5% of the time. That is, conceptual concerns as a criticism of the Confluent Program, are 10 times as prominent than in the "Best" features.

4.   Pragmatic issues apparently have roughly the same degree of concern as both "Best" and "Worst" features of this program (i.e., about one third of the total issues raised).

It is of note, given the apparent emphasis on "Gestalt work" in the program, *not one of the 40 respondents mentioned* it as a "Best" or "Worst" feature. This was initially puzzling to me, but perhaps Gestalt was subsumed under other categories, such as the opportunity to express feelings, personal development, and relevance to the needs of individuals.

Finally, it appears that criticism of the program by its own graduates (in this sample) is mainly conceptual; whereas, its greatest strength lies in people-related concerns. Furthermore, the "Worst" features were expressed in a somewhat more elaborate and divergent way than the "Best" features, which loaded on the people issues. These results from the "Best-Worst" study, in general, tend to confirm the results from the interviews of 16 administrator/faculty members—the major criticisms of Confluent Education in these two studies are apparently *not* the

Table 3.5

The "Worst" Features of Confluent Education Perceived by 40 M.A. and Ph.D. Graduates of the Program

Frequency	Rank for Frequency	Worst Features	Triadic Classification
16	1	Identity, definitional problems	Conceptual
14	2.5	Lacking in academic credibility	Conceptual
14	2.5	Not practical	Pragmatic
12	4	Features of the program per se	Pragmatic
7	5	Contradictory/paradoxical	Conceptual
6	6	Faculty quality	People
4	7	Student quality	People
Total 73			

people involved, but rather *conceptual* and *pragmatic* issues.

The Strengths and "Hang-Ups" Study

To complete the in-house studies on a critique of the Confluent Program at UCSB, in the spring of 1986 the author had gathered data from 26 students in a class named "Issues in Confluent Education." The data was collected within the framework of an exercise termed "Strength Bombardment" developed by Herbert Otto (1970). In this exercise, the students are instructed to first list the strengths of a person, activity, or program and then to list the "hang-ups" or blocks which might interfere with the actualizing of these strengths. In this

Table 3.6		
Summation of Data on "Worst" Features of Confluent Education		
Concern	Number of References	Percentage of References
Conceptual	37	50.9
Pragmatic	26	35.2
People	10	13.9
Total	73	100.0

case, the subject for these listings was the Confluent Program itself. The total lists (90 items) are too lengthy to include here, but some examples follow (see Tables 3.7 and 3.8). Table 3.9 summarizes the results from 46 listed "Strengths" and 44 reported "Blocks."

The main impressions from these data are listed below:

1.   It should be remembered that *all* these responses came from students then currently enrolled in this Confluent Education Program and ordinarily quite *biased in favor of this program.* (See OTL studies.)

2.   Here *people-issues dominated "strengths."* They are more than one half the total responses (52.2%).

3.   Conceptual and pragmatic strengths were perceived to be equal and, taken together, constituted less than one half (47.8%) of the total responses.

4.   "Blocks" were equally related to conceptual *and* pragmatic concerns. As in the "Best-Worst" study, "people" were *not* a major issue in "Blocks." "People" were cited only about 18% of the time, which is less than one fifth of the "Blocks" overall.

5.   The total number of "Strengths" and "Blocks" cited in this study were about equal, 46 and 44 respectively; whereas, in the "Best-Worst" study, the analogous numbers were 59 to 73.

Table 3.7
<u>Examples of "Strengths" Listed in "Strength Bombardment" Exercise</u>

Rich diversity of students.

It's fun!

Good blend of "hard-ass" scholarship and "touchy-feely."

People: The salt of the earth.

Intellectual challenge.

Emphasis on communication.

Accepting and patient when English is second language.

Real, usable (practical) information.

6. "Blocks," as in the "Worst" features in Confluent Education, expressed in somewhat more elaborated and divergent ways than were "Strengths" and "Best" features in the other study of the program. "Worst" features, again, were somewhat more frequently cited than "Best" aspects. "Worst" aspects were also more elaborated and more widespread than "Best" features of the program. In the interview study of 16 senior professors of education and administrators, there were *far more criticisms than affirmations*, possibly due to the primary question "How do you understand/account for what happened (elimination) to the Confluent Program here at UCSB?"

Data From Beyond UCSB

An important informational supplement for the critique and history of the Confluent Education approach came from *outside the UCSB campus.* This was a barrage of unsolicited, written comments from 47

Table 3.8
<u>Examples of "Blocks" Listed in "Strength</u> **<u>Bombardment" Exercise</u>**
Reputation, bad label. Program isolated. Elitist, middle-class, white, Anglo. Anti-intellectual orientation. MA program needs research course. Too much in the Confluent Lab Room. CE doesn't seem to exist outside of Phelps 2536 and so program lacks grounding in reality. Lack of young professors (no new blood). No process to transform feedback into action.

local high school teachers who were given the "Orientation to Learning" (OTL) instrument in the fall of 1985. The total OTL scores of this group were also of considerable interest as a part of several other studies comparing various reference groups on the OTL (Shapiro, 1984, 1985a, 1985b, 1985c). The OTL presumably measures degrees of a humanistic orientation to teaching and learning.

Originally 102 questionnaires were distributed to local high school teachers and 47 were completed and returned to the author, which is a respectable 47.8% return for a paper-pencil test—especially one with 90 items in a Likert-type questionnaire.

What took me *completely* by surprise was the great number and the hostility of the unsolicited comments written throughout the test on the test booklet itself. The test results per se revealed that the mean OTL score for those teachers who completed it was 287.7 on the OTL Form

Table 3.9				
Triadic Results of "Strength Bombardment" Exercise				
	Strengths		Blocks	
Concern	Frequency	Percentage	Frequency	Percentage
Conceptual	12	26.1	18	40.9
Pragmatic	10	21.7	18	40.9
People	24	52.2	8	18.2
Total	46	100.0	44	100.0

B1 B2 (90-item questionnaire). This is at the *22nd percentile* on the overall GSE norms *and* very similar to other OTL samples of experienced teachers in the public schools (K-12).

There were 71 issues from 51 comments by 47 teachers. A qualitative analysis of the comments follows in Table 3.10 and 3.11 (*Sixty-one percent of subjects who responded made at least one comment.*)

It is obvious to me that this (Table 3.10 and 3.11) constitutes *a powerful rejection of a humanistic philosophy* of education as expressed on the OTL, which represents a condensation of 100 pieces of writing by 89 outstanding authorities/scholars in the field of Humanistic Education. These OTL items, with the exception of one or two, were not my own statements. They also, *in no uncertain terms*, rejected the OTL per se, as a valid instrument to assess instructional values of high school teachers. There was much hostility directed toward the testing process *and* myself. Apparently, I was generally perceived as an "out-of-touch" and irritating academic. What surfaced was the unexpectedly high return/completion of 47 OTL questionnaires in a population of 102 high school teachers (almost 50%)—especially since so many were *so negative* about the process, content, and purpose of the OTL study. [It is important to note that spontaneous, unsolicited,

Table 3.10

Written Comments on the OTL by Local High School Teachers

Rank	Frequency	Percentage	Comments (Issues)
1	26	36.7	*Anger*/Frustration expressed mostly by *sarcasm.*
2	24	33.8	The *language* of the questions perceived as academic, out of touch, biased, meaningless nonsense.
3	9	12.7	*Hostility* directed at author and other "isolated" academics.
4.5	6	8.4	Impossible, impractical, *unrealistic* items.
4.5	6	8.4	Miscellaneous (e.g., these kinds of questions undermine teacher's authority, no *real* content, can't meet competitive demands, "laying on" guilt, advocating selfish individualism).
Total	71		

Table 3.11

Triadic Summation of Negative Comments on the OTL by Local High School Teachers

Concern	Frequency	Percentage
Conceptual	32	45
Pragmatic	25	35
People	14	20
Total	71	100

negative comments (or *any* comments) were *very* numerous here. Almost no written comments (positive *or* negative) were found in the hundreds of OTL tests previously and subsequently administered to other samples.] Many of the responses from the individual teachers follow:

[All italics are my own emphasis]

1. "I took time to read this and answer as best I could. I feel *uptight* and *used* by the content and language of this whole questionnaire. Statements are *loaded, biased, and contradictory.* Let's work *together!*"

2. "This like asking, "*Have you stopped beating your wife.*"

3. "Some of the items seem to be dictated by a *complete isolation* of the author from the realities of teaching in a typical high school."

4. "When your classes are *filled* with 30-35 students from *different backgrounds,* and some of your students have *no manners,* are completely 'spoiled' and expect to be entertained, you *must* establish your *authority* so that *some teaching* can be done."

5. "I would like to see *all education* professors take a *sabbatical* and *spend a year teaching* a full load of students at a typical high school, and they should teach at least two classes of underachievers."

6. "This survey sounds like the work of someone who has *never taught.* It reminds me of my theory classes at UCSB in the 60's. That

is *not the real world of teaching* high school. All these classes did *very little* to help me become a teacher. It is *difficult* to see *any value* in answering these questions."

7.   "I started to answer this (OTL) but, after a few questions, I realized this is coming from 'a dreamer in an ivory tower.' Come on out to the 'nitty-gritty' of the *real world*! Then you won't ask such *idealistic* questions."

8.   "Where's the follow-up for us?   This is too long and presumptuous to take so much of our time."

9.   "*Poorly worded, too 'confluent'* for those not recently into that jargon."

10.   "In general, I feel *supportive* of much of the philosophy underlying this questionnaire. However, I do have *concern* in the *implementation* or *interpretation* by teaching practitioners. We have been through an era of '*fun and games*' in education which left many students ill-equipped to cope with the *competitive demands* of an internationalized world."

11.   "The questions are *wordy* and full of educational and psychological *jargon* which makes them *very* difficult to give answers which truly represent my views. I *do not* wish *to be part* of this research."

12.   "I felt many of the statements were so couched in *educational* jargon that they were difficult to understand. The art of *plain writing* should be a goal of *all* education in my opinion."

13.   "These statements are *too vague* and hard to understand."

14.   "Too many *generalizations*. Answers different in different situations."

15.   "I really don't see how this can be of much *value*. It was *too long* and *too wordy* and very vague."

16.   "I hope this is *not* advocating a return to the UCSB or Isla Vista I *disasters*."

17.   "Wow!   You have used *loaded, emotional words* and terms in this questionnaire."

18.   "Typical 'educationaleeze,' wordings; *just awful*."

19.   "Whole thing is *garbage*."

There were also very brief comments (directed to specific OTL items) like:"Good grief," "Oh, brother," "This is silly," "Are you serious?," "Beware of Selfishness," "Is *that* maturing?," "Loaded question," "Is the real world *that* bad?"

Summary of the OTL Study with Local High School Teachers

The return rate in this study was a respectable 47.6%. There were a total of 51 unsolicited written comments on the OTL test booklets. These comments often covered several issues per comment and totaled 71 issues, nearly *all* of which varied from "*negative*" to *very* negative. There was only *one* initially positive comment, but even that response ended on a negative note. The content, form, and alleged purpose of the instrument, the educational philosophy it represented, as well as the study itself, were all *soundly* rejected.

The language of the questions, their perceived unrealistic character apparently *generated much hostility* toward the author, the OTL instrument, and the humanistic philosophy of education which it appeared to advocate. Actually, many of the teachers felt insulted simply by taking the instrument. Rather than dissipating their disapproval by "disagreeing" or "strongly disagreeing" with the statements as was called for on the test, *the degree of frustration and anger spilled out often in sarcasm and contempt expressed through the many spontaneous negative written comments.*

The anger and frustration engendered here covered *many* facets of Humanistic (or Confluent) Education (basic philosophy, wording of questions, socially regressive value advocacies, suggesting isolation from the "real world" of teaching, etc.).

Comparing the results of this study of high school teachers with the three in-house studies of general perceptions of Confluent Education and its program at UCSB by various reference groups, I conclude with Tables 3.12 and 3.13, comparative views of the results from all four studies.

From these tables, I conclude that:

1.   In the study of senior professors and administrators in the Education Department at UCSB, there were almost three times as many negative responses as there were positive responses in Table 3.11 (95 to 32 or 74.8% negative to 25.2% positive). This was a *very substantial, generalized critical response* from this group to the question "How do you understand what happened to the Confluent Education Program here at UCSB?"

2.   The negative responses were also *far more concentrated* than the positive responses. There were only six perceived negative categories of explanation, whereas, there were 21 widespread response categories

Table 3.12

Triadic Percentage Distribution of Negatively Perceived Features of Confluent Education in Four Studies

	1995-96 Senior Professors/ Administrators	1996 Best/Worst Per CE Grads	1986 CE Class	1985 High School Teachers
Conceptual	37.9	50.7	40.9	37.9
Pragmatic	45.3	35.6	40.9	45.3
People-related	16.8	13.7	18.2	16.8
Total	100.0	100.0	100.0	100.0

on the strengths of Confluent Education. In other words, perceived weaknesses were agreed on, but perceived strengths, far fewer in number, were also much more diffuse.

3. If students, teachers, administrators and professors could not directly contact, benefit from, or perceive the *positive "people effects"* of Confluent Education, apparently it lost most of its attractiveness and worth to the perceivers. As noted on the "strengths," "best features," etc., the overall impression of this program turns *very negative* when based largely on *both* conceptual *and* pragmatic grounds. However, in the Confluent "in-group" ("Best/Worst" features study), the "people effects" (warmth, affect, experiential teaching and learning, bonding expressive opportunities, a climate and community of trust and support, etc.) appear to strongly outweigh concerns about perceived pragmatic and conceptual weaknesses. These negative factors might have been recognized by the Confluent students and even more likely by the Confluent faculty, but were subordinated to the "humaneness" of the Confluent approach. It appears to be just the opposite for "outsiders."

On the negative side, conceptual weakness is *very* strong (almost four times as strong as "people concerns") (50 to 13). On the positive side, except for "outsiders," most of the studies show *conceptual*

Table 3.13

Triadic Percentage Distribution of Positively Perceived Features of Confluent Education in Four Studies

	1995-96 Senior Professors/ Administrators	1996 Best/Worst Per CE Grads	1986 CE Class	High School Teachers
Conceptual	34.4	5.1	26.1	
Pragmatic	31.2	30.5	21.7	
People-related	34.4	64.4	52.2	
Total	100.0	100.0	100.0	0

strength as not being very important (e.g., only about 5% in the "Best/Worst" study). This study was of students who graduated from the Confluent Program and were or are *nearly all* members of the UCSB Confluent community—ordinarily quite biased in favor of the program, according to OTL studies (Shapiro, 1997).

Apparently the major critique of the program from these sources were on conceptual and pragmatic grounds and the major strengths and best features were on people-related issues.

In House Critique from Books on Confluent Education

The triadic summary from *Advances in Confluent Education* (1996) by J. H. Brown, Editor is shown in Table 3.14.

As was so often noted, the persistence of identity confusion expressed by the questions "What is Confluent Education?" and "What does it accomplish?" was a significant critique in this book. The metaphoric nature of this term (Confluent), its vagueness and uniqueness, and lack of a clear and stable core concept were among the *many conceptual criticisms in this book* (71.4%). About one fifth

Table 3.14

Triadic Percentage Distribution
from Book Edited by J. H. Brown (1996)

Concern	Frequency	Percentage	Examples
Conceptual	20	71.4	Identity/Def(s), Significant weakness in conceptual core, no disciplined philosophical inquiry.
Pragmatic	5	17.8	Uncritical application from psychotherapy and psychology to education. Criticism of applications of "constructivism."
People-related	3	10.8	Lack of modeling, mentoring by professors.
Total	28	100.0	

(17.8%) of the critique was on pragmatic issues like general applicability and exportability. People-related issues were only three in number (about 10%) of the total critical comments.

The triadic summary from *Educating Our 21st Century Adventurers* (1996) by Phillip B. B. Moheno is shown in Table 3.15.

Again, in this book, conceptual issues (70%) dominate the picture of criticisms of Humanistic and Confluent Education and, again, a significant number of these comments concerned the weakness in the identity and definitions of Confluent Education and its lack of a central conceptual foundation.

Pragmatic issues were, again, a weak second (25%) to the conceptual critique and emerged mainly from empirical data (i.e., failure to confirm predominance of positive affect and clarity) from application

Table 3.15

Triadic Percentage Distribution
from Book by P. Moheno (1996)

Concern	Frequency	Percentage	Examples
Conceptual	14	70	Identity/Definitional, anti-intellectual, lack of empirical research.
Pragmatic	5	25	Classroom management issues creating negative affect and confusion in the students.
People-related	1	5	Teachers not well-trained to handle humanistic teaching.
Total	20	100.0	

of the HCIACS instrument to science and mathematics classes of practice teachers at UCSB. This involves classroom management—a pragmatic concern.

Finally, only one "people-related" critique emerged (5%) (Moheno, 1996, p. 57). This concerned the lack of preparation of the student teachers having a Confluent orientation to handle the sometimes disturbing side effects in the classroom.

In comparing the results from these two books, it can be seen that J. H. Brown's (1996) book, being a survey of current Confluent Education with 14 authors, was obviously more wide-ranging than Moheno's (1996) book. The latter had only one author and was an empirical study focused on the development of humanistic-behavioral measures of classroom behavior. In Moheno's book and Brown's work, the authors ultimately appeared to be in search of a basic model or coherent paradigm for Confluent Education. This, to me, is further evidence for the apparently persistent need to invent or discover a sound paradigm. It suggests that this task has not yet been accomplished.

The triadic summaries of critiques from both books were *very* similar in the order of the triads and the percentage distribution of criticism. To some extent, the analyses of these two books reveal somewhat similar orders of concerns as the four other studies. It appears that the major problem with Confluent Education noted in these books is perceived to be conceptual and, to a somewhat lesser extent, pragmatic issues. The problem is *not the people*—students and professors—but, on the contrary, the effects of "people-related" conditions are usually cited as the major strength of the program. Finally, the positive comments in both books examined were so numerous and so positive that both constituted a strong endorsement of the program and its effects. These positive comments were wide-ranging and far too many to enumerate.

Brief Analysis of The "I" in Science by Judith R. Brown (1996)

In this book, there were only a few hints of *any* limitations or negative critique. The entire book was presented as a powerful affirmation of the Browns' course, "The Role of Self in Qualitative Research" with its Gestalt Therapy, Confluent Education, and process-awareness foundation. To me, there *was little, if any, reflective consideration* of inner contradictions, limitations, or questioning of the epistemology of individual subjectivity. Therefore, there is no "triadic" analysis here. In these respects, Judith Brown's (1996) work was *substantially different from the other two books* reviewed for this critique.

According to Hart, who wrote the "Feature Review article" on her book for *The Humanistic Psychologist* (1996, spring), the strengths of the book by Judith Brown lie in generating fresh possibilities for qualitative research professors, the great value of experiential awareness in learning and, specifically, the skilled application and articulation of Gestalt principles to this learning process.

The weakness of the book, according to Hart (1996), lies in the singularity of the approach and the inadequate discussion of the larger context in which the self as researcher exists. Furthermore, while the Gestalt-Confluent training is considered valuable, it also has a ceiling and when researchers are wedded to *one particular view of reality*, other views are excluded. It is noteworthy that Hart sees this as the *central problem* which qualitative researchers *must consider* in their work.

The Original Humanistic Paradigm and Confluent Education

Human Teaching for Human Learning (HTHL) (Brown, 1971), the original comprehensive work on Confluent Education, in my view, is based on a somewhat implicit humanistic paradigm, as suggested by its title and other references (i.e., Preface, p. xii on "humanizing society," "the individual as an unique human being with enormous potential," "learning can . . . become more human," Editorial Introduction, p. xvi" . . . schools' lack of attention to the total needs of their students"). Also, from Editor's Introduction (p. xvi), "These (affective) techniques and disciplines derive from the *humanistic* psychology of such figures as Abraham Maslow and Carl Rogers." Note that "HTHL was derived from the Report to the Ford Foundation on the "Ford-Esalen Project in *Affective Education*" (this author's emphasis). George Brown states (Chapter 1, p. 3, Introduction and Rationale) that "Confluent Education is . . . sometimes called *humanistic* (this author's emphasis) or psychological education," also ". . . the extension of human consciousness and the realization of human potential" (p. 10). Above I say somewhat "implicit humanistic paradigm" because the specific adjective "humanistic" is *seldom* (this author's emphasis) mentioned in HTHL's 293 pages and leading figures in Humanistic Psychology (e.g., Bugental, 1963; Maslow, 1968; May, 1969a, 1969b; Rogers, 1961; Schutz, 1967), and Humanistic Education (e.g., Alshuler, 1969, 1973; Borton, 1970; Jones, 1968; Leonard, 1968; Simon et al., 1972; Weinstein & Fantini, 1970; etc.) are seldom introduced, except in passing, in the text and in the bibliography (p. 30). More and more Gestalt-Therapy techniques were being included in the program and as the program developed, the Ford-Esalen staff apparently kept increasing its contact with Dr. Frederick ("Fritz") Perls, the founder of Gestalt Therapy.

The Separation of Confluent Education from its Original Humanistic Base

Even though a specific humanistic paradigm was really not

developed, anecdotally the *effects* of the Ford-Esalen experiment appeared to be *very powerful*, and were reported in a style *bordering on religious testimonial* (this author's emphasis) (see G. I. Brown, 1971, chap. 7, p. 195). One of the most significant effects, in my opinion, was that the Confluent Education teacher-participants, having been "converted," more or less *completely substituted* Confluent Education for the older and much broader field of experiential, Humanistic Education. The latter is comprised of fields like sensitivity training, encounter groups, client-centered therapy, play therapy, psychosynthesis, explorations in positive experience, massage and body awareness, group-centered leadership, etc. So, the claims of *uniqueness* and the process of *separation* from other forms of humanistic approaches to psychotherapy, personal growth, and education began early as the advocates were caught up in a quasi-religious zeal. In my opinion, this resulted from their own ecstatic, affective experiences at Esalen and lack of experience with other humanistic approaches. What followed was a largely undisciplined, wholesale application of these techniques (especially Gestalt) to the schools. Limitations, reservations, social and individual, and consequences were probably not discussed very often or thoroughly by these newly converted enthusiasts if their writings presented a valid description of their beliefs. Possibly because of these conditions, only a weak conceptual base was developed as a frame for all this activity, energy, and affect. See Patterson (1973) and others (Child, 1973; Joyce, Hersh, & McKibben, 1983; Mosher & Sprinthall, 1971; Samples, 1970). Perhaps the framework was there, but much of it seems to have been implicit or vaguely stated in a Gestalt philosophy of education.

Problems with the Gestalt Emphasis in Confluent Education

Another problem with the emphasis on Gestalt Therapy in Confluent Education, almost from the start, was that the term "Confluent"[6] is metaphoric, ambiguous and problematic, and taken from a form of pathology in terms of Gestalt Therapy. This "Confluent" (education)

---

[6]The original label ("Confluent Education") for the Ford-Esalen Project was "Affective Education." The permanent label was suggested by Hillman in 1967, after over a year's exposure to the original Esalen-based program headed by Professor George I. Brown. See Hillman, 1973, pp. 18-26.

was not at all like Fritz's "confluence"—a pathological loss of ego boundaries and over-identification with other individuals, groups, or social movements.

It is important, I think, at this point in examining theoretical or conceptual grounding in the present also to trace the connection claimed by Perls, G. I. Brown and his followers between Gestalt Therapy and Gestalt Psychology. This alleged connection is important because so much of Confluent Education rests on Gestalt Therapy or "Gestalt Awareness," a protective and cosmetic term and probably "politically more correct" (safe) than "Gestalt Therapy." Perhaps Gestalt Therapy could claim more intellectual and professional respect if it were firmly based on Gestalt Psychology.

The Distinction Between Gestalt Therapy and Gestalt Psychology

In the first place, Gestalt Therapy as applied by Fritz Perls and his followers is not really much like the original Gestalt Psychology of figures like Köhler, Wertheimer, and Koffka, according to Gestalt scholars like Henle (1977), Arnheim (1974), Popplestone and McPherson (1988), and Coleman (1994).

Quoting from Popplestone and McPherson (1988, p. 150):

> The proponents of Gestalt psychology are gratified by the impact they have made, but they also find some recent references to the theory to be most unfortunate. At issue here is a misrepresentation, and one that appears to be spreading, that 'gestalt therapy' is an extension of Gestalt psychology. The former is an invention of Fritz Perls who extracted some of the terminology of Gestalt theory and transposed it inappropriately to variables related to psychiatric disturbances. Henle, an exceptionally sophisticated scholar of Gestalt psychology, reviews Perls' writings in the 1960s and 1970s and concludes: 'His work has *no* substantive relation to scientific Gestalt Psychology' (1978, p. 31).

Arnheim, a second Gestalt expert, also reacted in a strongly negative manner to a discussion of "Gestalt Therapy" in a publication of the American Psychological Association:

> It took me a moment to realize that the term *gestalt* in its precise historical and theoretical sense is losing its sanctuary even in professional journals"

(Arnheim, 1974, p. 570). Let the reader be warned ('caveat legens'): Gestalt psychology is a recondite, and thus often unfamiliar viewpoint in psychology, and references to it—even in learned circles—may deviate markedly from the actual concept.

From A. M. Coleman (1994, p. 1185), the following quote makes the very important point: "Gestalt approaches (to therapy) have not been subject to *any* (this author's emphasis) great amount of empirical research, which is in part, a consequence of the ethos of the movement and the *lack of precision* (this author's emphasis) in specifying models and methods."

Criteria for a Definition of Confluent Education

The defining term, label, or central concept of an approach to education or psychotherapy should be non-additive; that is, present a complete gestalt or a "confluent gestalt" as I will argue below. In my opinion, three criteria are essential for such a definition: (a) a philosophy (including an epistemology, values, and hermeneutics [interpretation]); (b) a method; and (c) a goal/outcome. To be most useful, definitions of what has been called "Confluent Education" should have met all three of the above criteria in an explicit way. For example, "Client-centered therapy" (Rogers) suggests an explicit method (focusing on the client's needs) and an implicit philosophy which includes the importance of the therapist's attitudes and sensitivity to the client's needs (especially the client's feelings).

"Humanistic Education," as a genre, fulfills all three criteria; whereas, the term "Gestalt Education" suggests a philosophy and method. "Integrative Learning" is a method and an outcome. Returning to the Gestalt lineage, perhaps the defining terms should be: Gestalt Psychology—> Gestalt Therapy—> Gestalt Education.

"Humanistic Education" could likewise be derived from Humanism (the philosophy): Humanistic Psychology—> Humanistic Therapy—> Humanistic Education. Behaviorism, as a psychology, would lead to Behavioral therapies, the implicit outcome of which would be changes (improvement) in behavior. Cognitive behaviorism is an additive, combined form as is Moheno's (1996, p. xv) reference to his instrument as a Humanistic/Confluent device.

Inherent Conceptual Problems in Confluent Education

In my view, there always have been conceptual problems inherent in the Confluent Education program/movement. The major problem is still the lack of an explicit, consensual definition—a more precise *internal* (this author's emphasis) understanding of what it included and what it did not include.

Apparently, these difficulties were not ameliorated by my study (Shapiro, 1975) on "Unpacking Confluent Education." Following this identity problem, there are demonstrable difficulties in transmission, application, explanation, and marketing Confluent Education. These problems, I think, prevented Confluent Education's ideas and techniques, many of which I regard as potentially very useful, from general diffusion into educational culture/society.

It has always puzzled me that other programs—even some innovative ones like the UCSB College of Creative Studies and the Public History program, also at UCSB, didn't *seem* to have such persistent, underlying definitional and explanatory problems, or, at least, I was not aware of them.

Speaking briefly of one of the outstanding institutional legacies of Confluent Education, the Norwegian "Meta-senter" for Confluent Education, Gestalt Therapy, and Psychosynthesis, I regard its name as a clear example of the additive problem in terminology and, therefore, in its central concept. However, in a significant part of Norwegian culture, at least, there didn't seem to be the deep definitional problem we had in American Confluent Education. I can't explain that apparent difference, except possibly in terms of how the Meta-senter programs were presented and the cultural readiness for such a seemingly culturally radical innovation. But even the name "Meta-senter" seems paradoxical to me because, by definition, a "meta" cannot be a "center," since the former is "above" any center. It is a position or way of viewing a "center" from a different level than its own. Perhaps, if the senter's main purpose were explained as a central place (institution) from which various personal growth methods could be studied from a "meta-position," the senter's current name would make more sense to me.

The Objects of Criticism by Confluent Educators:
The List of "Devils"

From four of the seminal books on Confluent Education (*Human Teaching for Human Learning*, 1971; *The Live Classroom*, 1975; *Advances in Confluent Education*, 1996; and *The I in Science*, 1996), the following is a list of *what is criticized most* ("the devils") (this author's emphasis) by the authors who all are or were leaders in the Confluent Movement.

1. Empirical (quantitative) research theory or data. (Note that Moheno, 1996, is *not* included here.)

2. Basic, traditional research in education (e.g., evaluation of specific curricula).

3. The "hard sciences," along with their methods like quantification, analysis, hypothesis testing, logical positivism, objectivity, linear thinking, etc.

4. "Instant" group leaders, not properly qualified. (With this criticism, I agree.)

5. Splits between theory and practice.

6. Scientists with "introjected," "top dog" demands.

7. Damning with faint praise (e.g., "empirical research has its place in education").

8. Any work or study which does *not* (this author's emphasis) deal with "real" reality (i.e., "the what and how of the here-and-now").

9. The study of values like social justice, especially in any philosophical or academic form.

10. Overt, explicit, political stands on any issues large or small.

11. Negative feedback (taken in the sense of criticism). Generally this was treated as a personal attack on the leaders of the program; hence, it was defended against vehemently.

Coercive Framing

Unfortunately, I detect considerable coercive framing in Confluent literature. The prototype for what I have termed "coercive framing" is "Heads I win, tails you lose." Another classical model of coercive framing is the core message, so common in various media commercials, "Ours is the *only* one, shouldn't you? Hurry right now!" The assumptions, conditions, and rules of coercive framing are all defined in such a way that the person, doctrine, issue, or event *compels a conclusion if* the party(s) being affected as the object of such framing actually "play the game," in terms which have been set by the framer. This is what some politicians do when they label the opposition as "extremist" or "liberal" or "socialist," etc. If the label sticks, the definition of "an other" place that "other" in an unwinnable position *if* (this author's emphasis) the party so labeled accepts this framing and especially *if* (this author's emphasis) an audience is already highly conditioned to agree with these labels. This is what is too often done in all kinds and levels of human relations. If one side can successfully define the terms or the way in which an issue is framed, it becomes impossible to "win" the contest (meaning having a desirable outcome for the one being "framed"). The term "framed" has, for many people, a familiar ring in the criminal sense, that is being setup for blame for the damage committed when the blamed person is really innocent. The rules, system, frame *guarantee* the outcome in favor of the framer.

One example of this is to be found in a foundational Confluent publication, the "Editor's Introduction" (pp. xvi, xvii) in *Human Teaching for Human Learning* (Brown, 1971):

> This is not . . . a traditional book on education. It is not the result of enormous scientific research; it is not a manual for teachers; it is not a theoretical treatise, nor is it the outline of a new curriculum. The state of the art of reinventing affective education makes the writing of such books premature. They will come later. Because *Human Teaching for Human Learning* is not in one of the traditional genres of education books, *it demands from the reader* (this author's emphasis) a special kind of close attention and involvement.

The editor does several things to set up the reader for coercive framing. First, the editor defines the book by what it is not, leaving a serious reader to then wonder what it really is and also tends to increase the book's value as a scarce resource. Second, the editor comments that the state of the art which this book demonstrates makes "the art of reinventing affective education (which is what the book proposes to do) cannot be done satisfactorily because the enterprise is premature." Hence, the reader's expectation is lowered so as not to expect anything like a precise exposition. Third, the editor reinforces that downsizing of scholarly expectations because this is not a traditional education book. And finally, given the above exclusionary definitions (what it isn't) and being *necessarily* incomplete, it would be wrong (premature) for the reader to expect more and, *therefore*, the reader is *required* (this author's emphasis) (I might say "coerced") into paying a *special kind of* close attention *and* involvement—not just any old close attention—a *special kind* (this author's emphasis) precisely because, by definition, the field is still somewhat vague.

The second example of coercive framing as *a feature of Confluent Education* also comes from a seminal book in the field, *The Live Classroom* (1975) edited by G. I. Brown.

In this book, the first tone-setting, substantive chapter is entitled "Gestalt and the Transformation," written by Geri Metz (1975)—an M.A. student in the Confluent program at that time. Geri was a specialist in teacher training in high school French.

Quoting George Leonard from his book *The Transformation* (1972), Metz (1975) reports on

> . . . the gift we give our children, the NDD: neurosis, disease, discontent. Many members of the medical profession acknowledge that up to *ninety percent* (this author's emphasis) of *all* (this author's emphasis) their patients' complaints stem from psychological causes and are not biologically induced. . . .

And after listing a litany of physical symptoms of mental illness adds,

> And we don't even mention the general unhappiness and discontent etched into the faces of civilized man, or the suicide, the broken homes, the ceaseless drive for more, the lack of satisfaction.
>
> The saddest part of this sad picture is that we accept most of it as the norm and that we allow society to perpetuate the sickness.

She quotes Perls (p. 20), "I consider that the basic personality in our time is a neurotic personality" (Perls, 1969, p. 30) and "neurosis is growth disorder." "Then the question shifts from the medical to the educational field" (Perls, 1969, p. 32).

From these very wide, exaggerated generalizations and claims, Metz (1975) proclaims (p. 20) "And while it is true that education is not therapy and teachers are not psychologists, it *should* (this author's emphasis) be evident . . . that we do need an educational process that is therapeutic and that is designed to lessen the NDD rather than contribute to it."

"*I am proposing Gestalt Therapy as a necessity for our age*" (this author's emphasis). She continues (p. 22) by listing many "new age" techniques and beliefs (e.g., extrasensory and psychic perception, astrology, occult traditions, LSD, provocative evidence for the intervention of highly developed beings from other planets visiting earth, etc.).

She (pp. 22-23) comes back to the educators who *must* (this author's emphasis) begin by reaching the teachers with Gestalt Therapy principles and states: "I am *convinced* (this author's emphasis) that these affective techniques . . . are vitally important to *every* (this author's emphasis) teacher and *must* (this author's emphasis) be a part of *every* (this author's emphasis) teacher's training *first for himself as a human being* (this author's emphasis) and then as a means of helping his students grow and realize their full human potential."

Metz (1975) ends (p. 23) with a paragraph, which again, reinforces the ideas that Gestalt Therapy principles, openness, uniqueness, awareness, and personal responsibility are *the only* (this author's emphasis) paths to fully realize human potential and can confront the NDDs. This will then help quicken the necessary transformation we are now undergoing.

In my opinion, this set of breathtaking proclamations from Metz is a classic example of coercive framing, which is matched in coerciveness and grandiosity only by her major professor's polemics in the "Introduction and Rationale" of his previous book (Brown, 1971, pp. 16-17).

The pattern (gestalt) of coercive framing consists of great promises *if* (this author's emphasis) you make the required choice, even though allegedly, you have complete freedom of choice. But you are "coerced" into making the *choice the gestalt authority requires* (this author's emphasis) you to make because the consequences are great rewards, if you submit, and disastrous negative consequences if you dare to reject this offer (e.g., G. I. Brown, 1971, pp. 3-18).

Unfortunately, as stated above, in my view, Confluent Education is permeated by coercive framing—sometimes in a rather mild and scattered way—perhaps without any conscious intention of harm or coercion. Other times the coercive framing seems both intimidating on purpose, however incongruent with the alleged premise of being "value-free" (see G. I. Brown, 1975, p. 296), the claim of authentic freedom etc.

Why is coercive framing especially problematic in an innovative, humanistic program like Confluent Education?

1.   Because we were and are on the defensive anyway and whether coercive framing is merely sensed or overtly identified in Confluent Education, this further weakens our credibility, I believe, because it is incongruent and hypocritical.

2.   Because some of the most significant implicit and explicit expectations reinforced in Confluent Education become repudiated by coercive assumptions or style, (i.e., the promises of authenticity, clear messages rather than double messages and truly being oneself) all can be compromised by coercive framing.

For example, it is my observation that people were told that they did not have to participate in any *affective exercises*, but the hidden consequences could be punishing and harmful if one significantly and consistently resisted the dogmas of Confluent Education, Gestalt, and group dynamics. Deviation from affectively participative norms were not well tolerated, in my view.

Double messages, the reflexive error, ambiguity, and hypocrisy are, of course, common in other academic programs, interpersonal relationships, in the media, institutions, and professions like mental health, politics, religion, the law, business, and public institutions, etc. But in Confluent Education, with its alleged high standards of confidentiality, personal confession and emotional expression, authenticity and fairness, to be disingenuous is particularly disturbing. That is so because that weakens the fabric of *trust*—so necessary in these fields—especially when violated by the "powers that be." And, finally, when trust or promises are violated it is often contagious in the client or student culture.

Lack of a Confluent Gestalt

The above notwithstanding, perhaps *the* most fundamental problem Confluent Education has had is that it lacked (for me and apparently many others) an *overall pattern* or coherence in design. It lacked a *"Confluent Gestalt"* (see Patterson, 1973, pp. 180, 187-188 and Iannaccone, 1996, pp. 171-173). Note that these two terms are *used profusely in nearly all the literature on Confluent Education but I have never seen the two concepts linked in this way.*[7]

Perhaps that's why one of my preferred metaphors for Confluent Education was "the creature," a kind of "jerry-built," patched together beast which is much like the proverbial "horse, designed by a committee."

Also, perhaps that is why in 1998 we are still pondering "WHAT THE HELL IS CONFLUENT EDUCATION?" and busy with additive solutions for the Confluent Education paradigm dilemma. This question was epitomized on one Confluent Education retreat in 1984 when badges (buttons) were passed out among the participants by the CEDARC group. This was an offshoot of the Confluent Education Program and was called the "Confluent Education Development and Research Center," which for a time held seminars, published a newsletter, and had some support. Its journal, *The Confluent Education Journal*, in some form, lasted for almost 10 years. However, in my opinion, it never had much influence on the pragmatic and academic aspects of the Confluent Education program. The circular badges read *"What the hell is Confluent Education?"*

I see this as a *deep symptom*—in this case, humorously presented—which reflects the *lack of a generally accepted and perceived overall pattern (or model) for Confluent Education* (i.e., for many, it was and is a mixed up, incomplete, non-Confluent Gestalt). Pieces could be seen/apprehended rather easily, but they never seemed to fit together very well neither cognitively nor perceptually. I think there were three basic indicators/reasons for this ill-fitting, somehow awkward "*Gestalt.*"

1. The name/identifying term *was both a misnomer* taken directly from pathology in Gestalt Therapy terms, and essentially metaphoric, so that many interpretations could be made of it. And its original grounding in Humanistic Education was therefore lost.

2. *Too many widely disparate approaches* were deemed acceptable. Evidence for this was the persistent statement (that I heard from students and faculty) of how *different* the original three faculty

---

[7]The one exception to note is in this book (pp. 9-10) in which Factor IV was derived from a multivariate content analysis of 89 experts in Humanistic Education. This is a label for this secondary factor emphasizing integration of affect and cognition in instruction. This was an empirically derived *advocacy*—not necessarily a description of actual conditions.

members were in their approaches to applications, teaching, research, and mentoring, and the same feeling/perception persisted both with the addition of Ana Reyes and Larry Iannaccone. I suppose I'm suggesting that almost *any* approach was acceptable *if* it included qualitative research methods, constructivism, affect, subjectivity, awareness, and individualism. So, from my perspective, if almost anything fits, nothing really fits (together).

The various courses, content, interests, and research methods were generally accepted by the students, but these methods and studies did not seem to hang together. To remedy this condition, we instituted a course entitled "Issues in Confluent Education," intended for a "grand synthesis" of the field, and I taught this course, but it was considered "marginal" and I agreed with that perception. The course was dropped after a few years. We kept changing our "tune" (e.g., Gestalt, Systems Theory, Neurotic Organizations, OTL). So both the melody and harmony were *disjunctive at a deep, conceptual/perceptual level.* And apparently this was true for many students and faculty and administrators within Confluent Education, and certainly for the Education faculty and other faculties and administrators not in Confluent Education, although none of them probably would state it in those particular musical, metaphoric terms.

There was a kind of internal disharmony which was perceived by the outside as "weakness," seldom discussed and acknowledged within the Confluent group but sensed and present, in my opinion, throughout the program's 27 years.

3. There was insufficient conceptual/dialectic discussion and discipline to unite the various pieces. *They never really fit together for us insiders* and, to me, we still have trouble explaining it to outsiders. This, I think, is so, though Confluent Education apparently had a profound effect on many students' lives, and it certainly influenced their professional work—many in a significant and positive way. It often changed and improved their personal and professional lives (e.g., relationships, research, and professional practices). The 1996 books and earlier (1975) and (1971) work by George Brown and others sought to document these assertions.

For some it was experienced almost as a "God-sent refuge" and for others a valuable but ultimately confusing experience, and that, in my opinion, is one of the reasons why it didn't survive as a program at UCSB.

Returning to the major metaphor for Confluent Education, the two (or three) streams *never did come together and become one inseparable river*—they stayed separate even though they probably flowed in approximately the same (humanistic) direction. Three conceptual streams, which I identify, were: The measurement research on the OTL led by myself, and Moheno's HCIACS versus the "Yoemans-Bloom Model" versus Gestalt Therapy as an all-encompassing theory and practice.

There was a disconnect between Confluent Education courses (labs) and actual practice in the field, as some of the comments on the "Strength Bombardment" exercise indicated in Chapter 3, pp. 73-75. And, finally, there was the M.A-Ph.D. *"GRAND CANYON EFFECT"* (i.e., huge gap) especially between the M.A. warm, personal attachments and sense of community, and the more isolated and intellectualized Ph.D. program, particularly regarding research demands, and the frequently impersonal atmosphere surrounding the Ph.D. candidacy.

Actually, we rarely ever went "into the field" together but instead brought the field into 2536 Phelps Hall at UCSB. People had very different undergraduate backgrounds (music, dentistry, theology, literature, art, poetry, social studies, counseling, biology, business, public relations, athletics, etc.). This variety is and has been held up as a virtue (see G. I. Brown, p. xi and L. Iannaccone, p. 167 in J. H. Brown, 1996). But probably because of it we lacked a common *disciplinary base*, which was not substantially compensated for by the course work or M.A. projects and Ph.D. dissertations. "We couldn't build a complete house without a solid foundation." To use the metaphor in a slightly different way: "We built a structure without emphasizing a foundation." We didn't have a firm disciplinary, research and/or philosophical foundation (see G. I. Brown, 1996; Hackbarth, 1996; and Kvernbekk, 1996), so our program collapsed when the pillars (senior professors) were removed. Apparently, the professors did *not* (despite their strengths) substitute for a foundation for this once very promising structure. Even educators like C. H. Patterson (1973, pp. 179, 189), who think that the ultimate goal of education is the production of self-actualizing person, contended that "Confluent exercises" are not necessarily clearly nor directly related to subject matter. Therefore, he observes, there is a *contrived* element present.

Patterson's (1973) critique of Confluent Education, in addition to the contrived nature of many Confluent exercises (often based on Gestalt techniques) includes the following points:

1.   The affective elements do not always appear to *"flow"* (this author's emphasis) from the materials of instruction (thus suggesting a "non-Confluent Gestalt").

2.   The Confluent method approaches direct instruction, using subject matter rather incidentally.

3.   Brown (1971, p. 96) provides no data to support his evaluation of the Confluent techniques as *all* (this author's emphasis) "extremely successful both in getting across the subject content and in getting the students in touch with their feelings."

4.   While nearly all the teachers in the Ford-Esalen project appeared to be enthusiastic about the classroom effects, such responses were not created by techniques.

5.   This whole aura (e.g., Ford-Esalen) is an example of the well-known "Hawthorne effect" in a classic study, showing that in an atmosphere of "good-intentions" almost *any* management intervention is perceived positively by the participants.

6.   The highly selective group of teachers and their impressive experience, competence, dedication, and enthusiasm introduces a strong teacher effect on the alleged outcomes.

7.   Exercises and games sometimes appeared to be over-emphasized rather than the teacher as a warm, caring, and responsive human being.

8.   Finally, the greatest deficiency in the Confluent method and most other affective education approaches is that they are not based on any systematic theory of human behavior of human development and interpersonal relations.

Apparently, the theory of Gestalt Therapy itself was not enough of a theoretical or philosophical basis according to Patterson. G. I. Brown, founder of Confluent Education, concurred in this view as recently as 1996 (Brown, 1996) "Recent Advances in Confluent Education," p. xiii.

The Assimilation Process

I understand the phrase, "to assimilate" to mean to incorporate, *subsume*, digest, dissolve, or break down something, so that it is indistinguishable from the "larger" whole into which it is assimilated.

So then, "new math" or focus groups, team learning, etc., when considered subsumed by Confluent Education, *lose* their unique identity and become examples of, or parts of, Confluent Education.

To "subsume" (assimilate) is to include *under* a more general class or proposition. The individual becomes part of the species. The species, in turn, becomes part of the genus, the particular is included *under* the universal, etc.

This "more general" class, proposition, or category is also considered a more comprehensive synthesis than that which is subsumed. So, "focus groups," etc. become subsumed *under* Confluent Education, as is "authentic communication," "being in the here-and-now," "being in reality instead of fantasy," etc.

By claiming ownership and credit for origination by Confluent people and Confluent doctrine, anything which is perceived to be remotely humanistic or humane is converted into an example of Confluent Education. This process is greatly facilitated by the lack of precision and conceptual boundaries inherent in the term "confluent education" or even Confluent Education.

The people, I and others *claim* to have observed, in this process usually begin in the sense of a "small c," noting the similarity of "confluent" ideas or practices with examples in the fields of teaching, consulting psychology, or psychotherapy. For example:

We're doing computer simulations, focus groups in Environmental Studies. It's interactive, like a play unfolding and "*That's confluent.*" or:

We're doing Distance Education Education in Geography with student teams. We have team conferences, with teams as far away as Utah and "*That's confluent.*" or:

"What do you mean 'demise'? All that 'new math' that's around, that's confluent. It's still out there, *all* around us."

Assimilation takes place in many fields, for example, "Take behavior, for instance. Well, we *all behave*, don't we? Therefore, we should all study *behaviorism.*" or:

"Motivation comes from the unconscious, and so all proper studies of motivation, by definition, belong in the *Psychoanalytic*/Freudian domain."

I see this "process of assimilation" as moving from a loose, general connotation (small "c" in confluent education) to a unique discipline/epistemology (capital "C") in two quick steps, in the case of

Confluent Education.
1.   We claim similarity in a general sense in "That's confluent."
2.   As we claim the name, we "own" the phenomenon. It becomes ours. We take credit for it. It becomes "assimilated" to our subculture, and the theory or practice in questions takes on a *capital* "C," with all rights and privileges of origination, authority, ownership, etc.

Again, "assimilation" is the process of converting anything perceived as even remotely interactive, humane, or humanistic (small "c") into the tacitly governing body or discipline of Confluent Education (large "C").

This is something like owning the mineral rights to a piece of property, no matter who owns the land, or like the sacred rights of burial grounds claimed by Native American people.

In the "assimilation process," I see several important symptoms of:
1.   A sign of our need for an all-encompassing uniqueness, involving profound disengagement from our historical roots and the rest of the humanistic field.
2.   An ineffective negative feedback loop for correction of this significant inflation. Just because many of us first discovered some of these methods in Confluent Education doesn't mean that we invented them!
3.   A self-enhancing, almost predatory, entrepreneurial orientation. "More is better." I do not, however, think this is a primarily conscious, deliberate or conspiratorial mechanism. I see it as a naive and defensive substitution of grandiosity for scholarly caution.
4.   We appear to have persistent problems of "confluence" (in the original pathological sense of gestalt) and "boundary" problems in open-systems terms.
5.   Unfortunately, these problems sometimes lead to grandiose inflation of the claims, concepts, and practices of Confluent Education, collectively and individually, and without credible evidence!

All too often, I have observed the typical comment, "That's confluent," instead of "confluent (or Confluent) is *that!*" The "that" in this sentence refers to something *much larger* than either the sense of confluent education or Confluent Education. It is the major premise of this book that our program has always been part of the genre of Humanistic Education which, in turn, is deeply embedded in the broad, societal scale, Human Potential Movement.

Conclusion: An Interpretation

I conclude this chapter with an interpretation rather than a conventional summary of the critique of Confluent Education detailed in the foregoing studies, book reviews, etc.

It is my contention that in 1975-80, starting with the publication of *The Live Classroom*, there was a historic but unacknowledged attempt to elevate the model of Confluent Education. This was a species (variant) upgrading of Confluent Education from the genus, Humanistic Education, to a new genus also called "Confluent Education." Confluent Education appeared to become more and more unique and our differences from rather than our similarities to other forms of Humanistic Education were emphasized. The latter was a genre with which Confluent Education was previously associated as a subset. Confluent was originally classified as (affective) humanistic, along with many other species, such as Values Clarification Self-Science, Curriculum of Affect, Progressive Education, Psychosynthesis as applied to education, and Student-Centered Education (Darling, 1994; Rogers, 1983; etc.).

This apparent paradigm shift was implemented by the above mentioned emphasis on basic differences (distance) rather than commonality with other species of the genus (general form) of Humanistic Education. Many of these alleged differences in the UCSB classrooms were based on principles of Gestalt Therapy to the extent that Confluent Education might have more properly been called "Gestalt Education."

In my opinion, however, Gestalt Therapy, as discussed above, was not directly derived from the original German Gestalt Psychology of Wertheimer, Koffka, and Köhler. As a *therapy*, it owed much to Moreno's Psychodrama and the organismic views of Kurt Goldstein (Anderson, 1983, p. 96). The term "Gestalt" (so often employed in most of the chapters in *The Live Classroom*) was used too loosely, was metaphoric and vague, and with many questionable attributions. The content and description of a "Gestalt" at a given time and situation was uncertain and indeterminate—a kind of mystical, catch-all term with *many* components, such as "here and now" (the *only* "real" reality), figure-ground awareness combined with body awareness and many and varied mini-experiments (exercises) with the clients (students). The issues of whether all Gestalten are the same, whether some are more ordered, inclusive or complete than others, and whether some have different effects than others were not discussed. Many other similar issues which *might* be better understood by analysis or at least reflection were also never discussed.

Since Gestalten were only vaguely defined, as in Confluent Education, many meanings could be given to Gestalt approaches to education, depending on the observer, therapist (teacher) and/or the subject (client-student).

The extraordinary claims of Confluent educators of the incredible power, depth, and scope of Gestalt-based techniques and processes were validated almost entirely by a quasi-religious epistemology of "true believers" and statements sealed by conviction and opinion rather than evidence. These claims were validated mostly by personal observation and highly favorable, selective quotes from the classroom, students and teachers. Hardly any scientific, empirical validation was provided.[8]

Thus, the "*development*" of Confluent Education was implied by nearly all of the original work cited in *The Live Classroom* (G. I. Brown, 1975) and recently continued in J. H. Brown's work in 1996. This, in my opinion, is development by "*elevation*," (i.e., over-generalization as to effects and applicability). The path and method of this new development (paradigm) was not based on analysis of the components or the interactions nor any visible dialectic process which might legitimately increase its depth and complexity. A coercive framing was and still is prominent.

The only part of the 1975 book which really challenged the all-out claims and paradigmatic elevation of Confluent Gestalt-based approaches came from George Brown himself, in the last chapter in the book, *A Cautionary Conclusion* (pp. 295-300), which has been discussed previously in this chapter. Steven Bogad, in his chapter in the same book elevating "process" to a new status (p. 159), nevertheless, did question the practice of "simply introducing affective components into the standard curriculum." He stated that he didn't believe that this tactic would achieve the Confluent goals of producing fully alive and integrated students and teachers. He also felt that "it is

---

[8]Shifflet and Brown (1972), Moheno (1996), and my own work on the OTL and TOTL (Shapiro, 1984-97) were exceptions.

indeed unfortunate that some of the attempts to "spread the word" of Confluent Education to teachers in the field have focused almost totally on developing affective techniques for current curricula." And, finally, Bogad conveyed his concern that "What we may end up with are new sets of written, prepackaged curricula, complete with cognitive and affective goals and techniques to be used in a school or classroom setting that do very little to promote the actual objectives of the material."

Along with the relative lack of dialectic thought and discussion, several other changes occurred during 1975-80, the period in which models and practices of Confluent Education were preconsciously elevated to a new status (i.e., a new paradigm). These changes were both significant and symptomatic of the internal view of this movement.

First, we cut off our relationship with other similar programs in academia such as the well-developed program in Humanistic Education at the University of Massachusetts. *Second*, Mark Phillips was removed from the "academic ladder" and "not allowed" to work with Ph.D. candidates on their research. He became a minor administrator. When he left the campus a few years later, we completely severed our operating connection with the University of Massachusetts group, previously our closest allies in Humanistic Education. *Third*, we replaced Mark Phillips with Laurence Iannaccone (who however distinguished, was not Confluently trained and never published any Confluent research). We shifted our major interest from the classroom to organizations and systems theory which were only vaguely connected to our original mission, which was largely applied to classroom teaching.

In so doing, as discussed above, we elevated our model of Confluent Education from a subset (species) of Humanistic Education with *many* common, basic components and instructional values and even techniques similar to other Humanistic Education approaches to a new genus/paradigm which emphasized *differences* rather than similarity. Thus, we isolated ourselves to a degree which I found destructive for our ultimate survival almost 15 years later, under the programmatic crisis of the retirement of the senior faculty and the difficulty in finding their replacements.

In practical terms, the cost of our isolation and claims of uniqueness (read "superiority") was that there was almost no visible pool of candidates to replace our *unique* and sometimes characterized as charismatic, three senior professors. The price of uniqueness and even distinctiveness was loss of connectedness with the larger movements of Humanistic Education and Humanistic Psychology and the rest of the entire Human Potential Movement. From these sources we might have been able to choose an academically qualified replacement. We couldn't find anyone who had similar instructional values, theories, and models and practices compatible with ours, but different enough to perpetuate the program and provide it with research skills and "new blood." Nor could we ever seem to produce a basic conceptual paradigm, understood by ourselves and our relevant reference groups. In my opinion, these conditions ultimately, along with the retirement of the three major professors, led to our demise in 1993 as an academic program at UCSB, *the* (this author's emphasis) major institutional/academic center for the development and continuation of Confluent Education.

Chapter 4

The Legacy of Confluent Education

If Confluent Education (according to its major metaphor) is like a merged stream of affect and cognition, it now (after over 30 years) has many outlets, some hardy and obvious, others hard to find in backwaters and swamps, and some completely dried up (like the Academic Program at UCSB, DRICE, CEDARC, etc.).

In a program involving over 400 (M.A. and Ph.D.) students from 1966 to the present time (fall 1998), it is very difficult to track all or even *most* of the outcomes and connections which form the legacy of Confluent Education. Suffice it to say, in this chapter I will select what I regard as some of the most prominent institutional, professional, and cultural reflections of its rich legacy.

In choosing the following four institutional exemplars of Confluent Education, I have been guided by four criteria:
1. Prominent Examples
2. Known to me
3. Accessibility
4. A demonstrable link with Confluent Education

Following case histories of these kinds of institutions and an analysis of their common values and diverse forms, I will move to the parts of the professional legacy of Confluent Education which are most visible and accessible to me. Some of the latter are the Special Interest Group ("SIG") in Confluent Education in the American Educational Research Association and the recently formed Association of Confluent Educators (ACE), with its widespread "chapters." The professional significance of these organizations will be discussed.

This will be followed by examples of a limited, but still vibrant, professional Confluent influence in a few classrooms in the elementary schools in the Santa Barbara area. However, these do not represent, by any means, institution-wide legacies.

The final legacy to be outlined here lies in the cultural domain, by far the most difficult, subtle, and complex field to document. This is so because the cultural/contextual effects of Confluent Education are diffused in many ways by a kind of "ripple effect" throughout this society and others. These effects are almost impossible to separate from the larger, overall impact of the Human Potential Movement per se, in which Confluent Education is assumed to be deeply embedded. And interwoven are the effects of other closely related programs and movements, such as Affective Education, Humanistic Education, Humanistic Psychology, Group Dynamics, Gestalt Therapy, Neuro-Linguistic Programming, and the Mental Health Movement in the United States and Europe (see Figure 2.1, Chapter 2 on The Origins of Confluent Education).

Institutional Legacy

My four examples of the institutional legacy of Confluent Education are:
1. The Santa Barbara Middle School
2. The Pacifica Graduate Institute
3. The Concord Institute
4. The Meta-senter for Confluent Education, Gestalt Therapy, and Psychosynthesis

Each of these examples will include a current description of the institutions, the story of their development from their origins to the present time, their links with Confluent Education, and my interpretation of each example.

The Santa Barbara Middle School

Current Description

Located on the former campus of St. Anthony's Seminary in the foothills of the Santa Yñez mountains, the "Middle School" (as I will refer to it) is a western American, suburban, private, alternative school for grades six through nine. Metaphorically, I see it as a unique "Traveling Bicycle Tribe," modeled on Native American cultures from the "four corners" area of Utah, Colorado, Arizona, and New Mexico (mostly Hopi and Navajo). It has grown from a very small school founded in 1976, with a budget of approximately $20,000, in downtown Santa Barbara, with 22 ninth grade students and three faculty into a much larger facility. As of the fall of 1997, it will have 170+ students, over 30 faculty, and a budget approaching 2 million dollars.

Among the many outstanding activities of this unique school, the "Rites of Passage" trip taken in June 1997 epitomizes its deeply humanistic philosophy and methods. The following is my slightly edited version of a quote taken from an oral history interview with its Headmaster, Kent Ferguson, assisted by Jill Wallerstedt, his public relations associate. This ritual takes the place of traditional graduation ceremonies:

> "Rites of Passage" is literally a day of words, a day of poetry, a day of music, and for 20 years this has been going on. Margot Kenley, the founder of the school in 1976, initiated this ritual and any child can't officially leave the school without finding someone who, in his/her behalf, will get up, in front of hundreds of people, and speak about the growth of this particular child.
>
> The witness, who stands up, will *not* talk about whether this youngster got a B+ in French or an A- in Math. The "witness" will talk about what the student has overcome and whether he/she is fulfilling his/her destiny, his/her humanity of what this person is inside, and to what principles has he/she been true.
>
> Then the faculty will write a poem, and flowers are fastened onto the child. This is like a diploma in other schools. This is a community "happening," a community celebrating its own and its childrens' "coming of age."
>
> When we are on bike trips or overnight hikes during the last 3 weeks of the year, before the Rites of Passage, we have, in a way, prepared the children by our "four corners" trips on which we make things and compare them with things made in another culture. For example, the Hopis' Kachina Dolls. We then go to art, geography, making a newspaper, comic strips, science fair projects, rock art, bookmaking, and chemistry.
>
> All of this is so packed together that there are not distinct disciplines. It's like a "hodge-podge." Here, in my room, there are products that show that we can deal with chemistry, math, science, anthropology, gardening, bicycle mechanics, mysticism, computers, and recycling materials. And some of the kids do research and write up their results, making a 180 page textbook for the next trip to the four

corners area.

And once all this is done, the kids take off on a pilgrimage which is called the "Rite of the Wheel," which pertains to the bicycle wheel and also the Buddhist "Wheel of Life" and the "Medicine Wheel." So we're off for 17 days, 20 teachers, 70 kids, but we also have 5-year-old children, dogs, and parents because we are creating a *tribe*--an extended family situation. Every night the tribe comes together to sing songs written by the tribe and recorded by the tribe, so that you can learn your tribe's ways. Sitting by the fire you will hear some stories, ancient mythological ones about the whole world, just like the ancient people would have done.

Finally, the night will close by a teacher or parent simply saying, "we are now going to go to our left. We are seated in a circle. Anyone who wishes to share something, complain about something, but mostly *honor* something, put up your hand. We're only going around once, then we're going to bed." This, in a way, helps prepare for the "Rites of Passage."

But before any child can be in the "Rites of Passage," he/she must have done thousands of math problems, read hundreds of pages, written hundreds of pages, and be computer literate. He/she has also studied a foreign language, studied history, and has had 4 years of science by the 9th grade. And many have been in drama and athletics.

There are many other current features which reflect the philosophy of the Santa Barbara Middle School, but space considerations of this book limit me to only a brief reference to some of them. First, its only formal statement of the philosophy of the school is a brief (two pages) document.

This statement includes a review of the founding of the school, generated by the concerns of a group of parents, teachers, *and* students. All agreed that the junior high school years are crucial for the development of creative, interpersonal, and academic skills. However, this group, along with Margot Kenley, the founder of Santa Barbara Middle School, considered these years the weakest link in the educational chain.

The goals, purposes, and methods to address this situation are portrayed as follows:

1.   Provision of a challenging, structured, yet innovative, academic environment--a solid foundation for later achievement.
2.   Instruction for adult responsibilities in career paths, friendship

patterns, peer pressures, and special issues.

3. Opportunities for the expression of creative and artistic talents and interests (e.g., drama, music, fine arts, computers, video production, and photography).

4. A respect for the natural environment by extensive hikes and bicycle trips which also emphasize other cultures, especially Native American culture, responsibility, and physical fitness.

5. Meaningful and sustained communication with the families of the school by frequent newsletters, town meetings, and contacts between families and staff on the progress of each student.

6. Provision of an environment in which the balanced development of the whole child is paramount. We see all human beings, including middle school children, as thinking, feeling, moral, social, and spiritual beings. There is no specific religious orientation, but the endeavor to find truth in each and all spiritual paths is central to Santa Barbara Middle School.

The Story

As mentioned above, the Santa Barbara Middle School was founded by Margot Kenley in 1976. At that time she was an M.A. student in the Confluent Education Program at UCSB. With the help of some parents, friends, and advisors, Margot actualized her mission in the form of an intervention in the usual sequence of education for junior high school students. The Santa Barbara Middle School was formed to replace the often problematic public or private education in these critical years with a supportive, personalized experience.

With the help of a group of interested parents and others who formed the board and a few interested teachers, the school began in a very small classroom facility owned by the Santa Barbara Unitarian Church in downtown Santa Barbara.

The first year of the school's student body consisted of 22 ninth grade students, and only three faculty. These students graduated after 1 year at Santa Barbara Middle School. Among Margot Kenley's advisors was Kent Ferguson, a UCSB doctoral student in mathematics and history and a certified teacher in math and social studies.

After a few years, it became apparent to Margot and others that being an administrator was very difficult for her, partly because it took her time and energy away from what she loved and excelled in—the creative teaching of English.

In 1980, the board, reacting to Margot's acknowledged "burnout," terminated her contract and both the board and faculty chose Kent Ferguson as her successor. He had become a very successful, charismatic teacher of social studies. Margot agreed with this choice and passed on her "baby," as she called it, to Kent for safekeeping, nourishment, and growth. Kent accepted the position and changed the title to "Headmaster" from "Director," which it had been labeled previously.

Kent was chosen openly by both the board and the faculty—an unusual pattern of succession, in that usually only a board chooses the Headmaster in private schools. Kent apparently received strong support from both groups because they had seen his success and popularity with the children at Santa Barbara Middle School, and he had the proper credentials and experience.

In 1980, Kent began what has become, to date, an 18 year journey as Headmaster.

The Link with Confluent Education

According to the Santa Barbara Middle School's *philosophy of education,* the purpose of schooling in the middle years is not merely nor even primarily academic achievement (i.e., appropriate subject-matter knowledge and cognitive skills per se).

It is the major purpose of the Middle School to develop the *whole* child—including building a constructive, socially-oriented value system, cooperative rather than competitive values, and strong community identification within the school and with the surrounding communities.

This purpose also includes much physical challenge (e.g., 600 mile bike trips) with peer support, productive democratic relationships with teachers and other adults, and probably, above all, the type of peer respect which is so often missing in traditional public and private schools in the early years of adolescence.

Subject matter learning is not neglected but far more broadly conceived than in most middle schools. Drama, poetry, music, personal growth, respect for other cultures and other people are emphasized—not simply grades and tests.

In addition, the scope, and depth of activities which are integrated into the curriculum are beyond the usual curriculum advocated in Confluent

Education, and even far beyond the individual-centered, directly psychological, personal growth aspects of Confluent training.

Although Margot Kenley had been influenced, in a general way, by the instructional values and teaching methods of Confluent Education at UCSB, the Santa Barbara Middle School was not envisioned as a specifically confluent school. Nevertheless, the underlying values and practices are congruent with Humanistic Education and, therefore, congruent with Confluent Education. More specifically, Kent Ferguson shaped the school, along with the faculty and board of trustees, according to his own vision—a traveling "tribe-like" school, guided by what he calls his "dream" or "the experiment."

Interpretation

In my view, the Santa Barbara Middle School has been deliberately modeled on protypically high-context cultures, like Native American and, to some extent, on Eastern religion and mythology—all based on an outdoor and tribal foundation to a degree which marks this school as unique. It is a humanistic, supportive ambiance, combined with academic excellence, and, in my opinion, it has been developed quite beyond the scope of many humanistic or confluent private or public schools.

To me, after considerable study and analysis, there still remains a certain mystique about this school. I can't quite see, for example, how they can maintain their apparent academic excellence with all the normally extra-curricular activities, like long bike trips, community service, and "rites of passage" etc. Maybe their "secret" lies in their teachers' ability to make each situation a vital learning experience, and most often, meaningfully connected with academic knowledge and personal and collective development.

Perhaps some mystique is inevitable when a small middle school is headed by a "*tribal visionary*" like Kent Ferguson.

The Pacifica Graduate Institute

Current Description

The Pacifica Graduate Institute, a Santa Barbara school offering M.A. and Ph.D. degrees in psychology and mythological studies, recently has been granted accreditation by the Accrediting Commission for Senior Colleges and Universities of the Western Association of Schools and Colleges. This is an institutional accrediting body recognized by the Council on Postsecondary Accreditation and the U.S. Department of Education. The Institute's President, Dr. Stephen Aizenstat, announced the accreditation on June 27, 1997, saying that everyone involved with Pacifica feels deeply affirmed by this recognition of their academic community. With this achievement, Pacifica Graduate Institute joins UCSB, Westmont College, and Fielding Institute on the local roster of WASC-accredited senior colleges and universities. The report of the site evaluation team included the following: "[we were] deeply impressed by the quality of education that has been carefully nurtured at the school and the spirit with which this particular learning community goes about fulfilling its mission."

Pacifica offers graduate degree programs grounded in depth psychology, following some traditions of Freud but primarily those of Jung. Since acquiring a new campus in 1989, the Institute has restored and renovated existing buildings and completed new construction in the same Spanish architectural style. The grounds have been extensively re-landscaped with drought tolerant plants indigenous to this climate zone. With a faculty and staff totaling over 80 people, Pacifica is one of the major employers in the Carpinteria Valley. There are 400+ full time, weekend residential students.

Pacifica's students, who travel from throughout the United States and Canada, are in residence each month when classes meet during three-day retreat sessions. Core faculty are joined by visiting scholars distinguished in the fields of psychology, literature, and religious and mythological studies. Pacifica offers public conferences and continuing education courses in addition to its graduate degree programs.

Classes are held at the Institute's 15-acre retreat-center campus in the Santa Barbara foothills, overlooking the Pacific Ocean and the Channel Islands. Surrounded by oak and eucalyptus groves, the historic-estate campus allegedly offers a unique setting for contemplation and study.

Pacifica's campus goal is to move toward a model of environmental sustainability in keeping with the Institute's dedication to tending soul *in* the world and the soul *of* the world. It is their belief that in addition to their academic studies, students will receive an education by the experience of being on their campus—an invitation to bring a more ecologically-oriented lifestyle into their everyday lives.

Diverse Student Backgrounds

Students at Pacifica Graduate Institute come from many parts of the United States, Canada, Central and South America, as well as Europe, Asia, and Australia. Each month, they travel from their home communities to the Institute's Santa Barbara campus to participate in the three-day class and study sessions.

Reaching Pacifica at a wide range of ages and life stages, students bring with them the richness of a broad spectrum of backgrounds and experiences. The Institute encourages a student community which reflects the multiplicity of the human imagination and fosters an environment which is culturally sensitive, appreciates cultural, racial, and ethnic uniqueness, affirms diverse lifestyles, and is open to values across cultural lines. The students reflect diverse disciplines as psychotherapy, education, medicine, performance arts, architecture, ministry, politics, writing, cinematography, and environmental studies.

The Mission of Pacifica Graduate Institute

Pacifica traces many of its central ideas to the heritage of ancient storytellers, dramatists, and philosophers from all lands who recorded the workings of the imagination. The legacies of these early men and women have evolved through a long succession of teachers, poets, novelists, and scientists—ultimately leading to the systematic explorations of the unconscious by Freud, Jung, and other theorists of this century.

The late mythologist Joseph Campbell was a strong supporter of the school in its early days, often offering special lectures in the Institute's public conferences program. In 1990, his widow, Jean Erdman Campbell, decided to place Campbell's archives and library at The Center for the Study of Depth Psychology, which is housed on the Pacifica campus. In making this decision, she said that [Campbell] "felt this is the place that would take his work, especially the study of the psychological meaning of mythology, into the next century." Before her death in 1994, Marija Gimbutas, professor emeritus of neolithic archaeology at UCLA, also decided to place her personal research materials at Pacifica, thus expanding the Institute's educational and research resources.

The presence of the Campbell and Gimbutas archives has attracted other significant collections to the campus and led to the Institute's establishment of master's and doctoral programs in mythological studies framed in the traditions of depth psychology that same year. Renowned depth psychology author James Hillman has placed his working archives at the campus. In 1996, Pacifica added a Ph.D. in Depth Psychology to its programs. All of the Institute's degree programs seek to contribute the gifts and insights of the human imagination to the personal, cultural, and planetary concerns of our era. This dedication is contained in Pacifica's motto: *animae mundi colendae gratia* (for the sake of tending soul in the world).

The Institute offers three graduate programs in psychology:
1.   A Ph.D. in Depth Psychology
2.   A Ph.D. in Clinical Psychology
3.   An M.A. degree in Counseling Psychology

All of these programs have a depth psychological perspective and each is recognized and approved by the State of California. In addition, graduates in Clinical Psychology are eligible to apply for California State Licensure.   Counseling Psychology M.A.s qualify for the Marriage, Family and Child License (M.F.C.C.). All of these degree programs are multidisciplinary, attempting to integrate the study of the humanities with traditional courses in psychological research and clinical practice.

The Story

This school had its roots in the 1970s in a community counseling center in Isla Vista and, operating as the Human Relations Institute, began offering State-approved master's degrees in counseling psychology in the early 1980s.   A Ph.D. program in clinical psychology was inaugurated in 1987. In Stephen Aizenstat's (founder and president of Pacifica) own words (slightly edited),

> After a year or two I became an administrator and a counselor in the Isla Vista center because the administrator left. I think my position was probably by default, but that was the beginning of the trajectory of my role as President or Executive Director of an agency.
>
> So, that developed and evolved. Years went by and I then included Gary (Linker) the second or third year I was there. I met him in the Confluent Program. We moved closer to the University to another

location on Hollister. There we initiated the first *real seedling* of what became Pacifica.

We were still educators, so we were always into *teaching* how to become a therapist. So we developed a certificate in counseling skills. We did that for many years and then that was the entree to approach the State that became the *approved Master's Program in Counseling Psychology.* I then started getting increasingly interested in the spiritual dimension and went to Esalen. I continued at Esalen, learning spiritual approaches like Psychosynthesis and other transpersonal ways of helping people.

Then I discovered James Hillman's work at Esalen, especially his book, *Revisioning Psychology*, a whole Jungian imaginal archetypal approach to psychology. This just "knocked my socks off." I think that was a turning point in my life in 1985 as was George Brown's first book *Human Teaching for Human Learning* in the early 1970s.

And then right from Esalen, I went into the Wright Institute (Berkeley, California), where Hillman was giving a series of lectures. I listened and could only understand about 10% but was totally inspired. Hillman came up with the idea *"animae mundi"* (soul of the world) which I incorporated into our later motto ("For the sake of tending the soul in the world").

This ideal was the intersection of social service and world-view psychology. Since I have always been a social activist and since I was a teacher and since I was now a therapist, to find the *intersection* (confluence) of those disciplines was really extraordinary. . . .

Then—so, then it became our big question in about 1985: Do we set up a new non-profit organization, or a proprietary organization profit-making? I had now gone to get my Ph.D. in Clinical Psychology at Fielding Institute and I was involved in all of what happened at Fielding, which had to do with the two founders at Fielding completely getting critically rejected by their board of trustees.

But I thought, "if I'm gonna' make this and move with a vision, do I really want to get caught in this 'web' again—yet another board of trustees, another set of battles?" Then I became clear in my vision. I had a sense, clearly sharpened in my "mind's eye," of what I wanted to accomplish in a school, with this mission so clear and precise that nothing would endanger it.

I was just now old enough to appreciate (in my 30s) the actualities of the world and how hard it is to really move with something and allow it to endure, because everything gets so compromised and so manipulated. You know, there are so many interests pushing and pulling.

So I decided to interview six or seven college presidents and asked, "If I were to found a school, how would I do it?" And each and every one of them said "The one thing I would *not* do, is to go back into a non-profit structure. The reason for that is that there are so many forces that happen with boards of trustees that you're never certain of the outcome. If you're really intending to complete this mission, make it a proprietary school."

That was totally alien to everything in me. My dad was a public school teacher, his dad was a public school teacher, I was a social activist. I went through a year of psychotherapy, a year of reflection on this decision because I had, in myself, I had it that "proprietary" = capitalism, exploitation, money. None of that was worked out, at all.

So, that became one of the most helpful lessons: To understand the relationship between money and psyche and self-worth. What's the "shadow" of it? The whole thing? And then I came down on the side of proprietary, but it was a *modified proprietary* system, which is what Pacifica is. It's proprietary in the bottom line but it's still not *fully proprietary* and it's not fully a non-profit institution.

So that started moving and then the next big event happened. We were operating classes at La Casa de Maria. That was nostalgic for us because we had our orientation toward Confluent Education there. And that's also where the Fielding Institute held their orientations and oral doctoral exams.

We just got too big and La Casa wanted to boot us out. We looked all around for a new home and finally landed here, and that was about 9 years ago (1988) and that really simplified things. Then we started our development as an institution with the primary advocacy and mission rooted in depth psychology.

It's kind of a socially conscious corporation, which I think combines the *best* of the proprietary plan with the *best* of the non-profit form. It creates a *hybrid*, so to speak. The services are managed by a board of trustees. They have full fiduciary responsibility. I am a salaried employee here and, at the same time, I have ownership rights. This means that in a serious crisis—and I trust my own intuition here—if I saw it going off my vision, I would have the capability of making an "adjustment." And also I am guaranteed that it doesn't go beyond me—*after me* comes the board, for succession.

I see the universities turning more and more to the private sector to help finance, etc. Even places like Stanford are involving high tech industries in supporting it. So there is a whole momentum, moving towards proprietary and away from state-subsidized, non-profit institutions. So now there's a lot less adversarial energy toward this new approach.

The Link with Confluent Education

Stephen Aizenstat, along with Gary Linker, were the most influential and had the closest link with Confluent Education in the evolvement of the Pacifica Graduate Institute. Both received their M.A. in Confluent Education in the mid-1970s and both had been humanistic teachers in public schools and were, therefore, quite likely open to a number of different Humanistic/Affective Education graduate programs. Apparently, their choices to attend UCSB in particular, were more expedient than substantive.

Most of my impressions of the relationship between Confluent Education and Pacifica come from my two extensive interviews with Stephen Aizenstat, the founder and president of Pacifica from its beginning in 1988. These links and some divergencies are summarized below:

1. First, the central mission of Pacifica rests on the belief that human experience is diverse and multifaceted. Therefore, its entire curriculum is interdisciplinary (Confluent?), and its student body is very diverse in background; although, as in Confluent Education, there is a significant concordance of values in faculty, staff, and students. They are very humanistically and especially spiritually oriented.

2. Aizenstat's "discovery" of James Hillman at Esalen parallels George Brown's "conversion reaction" to Fritz Perls and Gestalt Therapy, also at Esalen. These events became foundational to both the Confluent Education Program at UCSB and the Pacifica Graduate Institute. And they both came from Esalen, the prime embodiment of the Human Potential Movement. This, again, strongly reinforces my impression of the Confluent Education Program as being deeply embedded in the Human Potential Movement. This is the key premise of this entire book (if this movement, is, in turn, recognized as part of the world-wide historic "Humanistic Impulse").

3. Even though its president repeatedly refers to the "confluence" of many features of Pacifica, the current mission of this institution is anchored in Jungian depth psychology, which is quite different from the primarily Gestalt origins of Confluent Education.

4. It is my impression that, aside from powerful germinating and inspirational forces directly from Confluent Education, these are

(allegedly) reflected in the *way* they teach at Pacifica, rather than in their mission. I am not certain how this specifically confluent influence manifests itself in their teachers. I think there could be wide variance in these practices.

5.   In spite of these possible limitations of the influence of Confluent Education on Pacifica, on the deeper philosophical levels (e.g., spirituality, mythology, mysticism, study of the classics, etc.), Confluent doctrine and practices are still considered by its president, as one of Pacifica's "deepest taproots." (Both programs created high-context subcultures.)

6.   The significant divergencies between these two institutions seem to me to be:

(a)   The secular humanistic religion/philosophy which has remained as the basis of Confluent Education, at Pacifica is displaced by deep spirituality. Jung is the "godfather" of Pacifica. With Confluent Education, Perls is the "godfather."

(b)   The integration of classics and humanities (especially mythology and archetypal psychology) with modern, western clinical and counseling psychology. This level and kind of integration was almost entirely lacking in the Confluent Education Program.

(c)   The somewhat anti-intellectual, individualistic tone I saw and experienced in the Confluent program is not evident at Pacifica.

My main conclusion regarding Pacifica's link with Confluent Education is based on the fact that Confluent Education came earlier in the lives of Pacifica's founders (early to middle 20s). The 1970s were obviously times of turbulence, stirred up by the Vietnam War and the flourishing counterculture. Probably, at that time, "Steve and Gary," the young idealistic teachers, would have been also receptive to a wide range of Humanistic Education/Psychology programs other than Confluent Education. Therefore, although the link between Confluent and Pacifica remains substantial and, to some extent, formative, in my opinion, the *particular influence* of Confluent Education is overshadowed by the profound cultural changes at that time. These were best characterized by the broad Human Potential Movement itself. It was the "Movement" that mattered most, not the "Program."

Interpretation

The Pacifica Graduate Institute has much in common with the Santa

Barbara Middle School in that both are conceived of as high-context subcultures. And although obviously different in level of instruction and having developmentally different emphases (junior high school versus adult graduate school), the basic cultural similarities are much more striking to me than their differences.

First, both have visionary leaders. In Santa Barbara Middle School I see Kent Ferguson as a tribal visionary, whereas, in Pacific Graduate Institute, I see Stephen Aizenstat, founder and current president, as *an entrepreneurial, depth-psychology visionary leader*. That these are both inspirational visionaries and that both have deliberately built high context-institutions is not an accident. Stephen Aizenstat helped Margot Kenley set up the by-laws of Santa Barbara Middle School, and Kent Ferguson was on the board of the Pacifica Graduate Institute. In addition, Aizenstat's son is about to enter Santa Barbara Middle School this coming fall.

Their stories reveal rapid growth after an initial schooling of the founders in Confluent Education. Both began very modestly. Santa Barbara Middle School now has a budget approaching two million dollars, and Pacifica Graduate Institute has a current budget of approximately six million dollars.

The constant addition of programs, faculty, facilities, and community support shows a striking similar pattern. Both institutions pioneered some unique patterns in their respective forms. Pacifica is more directly spiritual than Santa Barbara Middle School and Santa Barbara Middle School is much more of a traveling, outdoor school. But both are radically alternative in their statements of mission and methods of instruction.

Pacifica has demonstrated its uniqueness in many ways, as has Santa Barbara Middle School. The former has accomplished this in its structure as *both* a proprietary *and* non-profit institution, in its emphases on depth psychology and mythology, and its acquisition of invaluable resources like the Joseph Campbell and Marija Gimbutas archives.

In addition, perhaps the most prominent feature of both schools is their profound humanistic orientation. In Santa Barbara Middle School, a central metaphor for this is the simple "log in the woods." On one end is the teacher and on the other is the student—on an equal plane, not one elevated over the other and in a one-to-one bonding interaction.

In Pacifica, the courses are taught with experiential components geared to the personal and spiritual growth of the students. In theory, at least both are highly "confluent" in the broadest sense of caring for each individual, emotionally, intellectually, and spiritually.

The link of Pacifica with Confluent Education is, perhaps, more explicit than the link for Santa Barbara Middle School in that both Stephen Aizenstat (president) and Gary Linker (former vice-president) completed their M.A.s in Confluent Education.   According to Aizenstat, his Confluent experience continues to inform his practices at Pacifica to this day.   For example, Aizenstat uses some Gestalt techniques like foreground and background exercises, being in the "here and now," and contact-withdrawal demonstrations. Apparently he also relies on many group process approaches learned in Confluent Education.

In a very general sense, these two unique and, to me, very impressive institutional legacies of Confluent Education have demonstrated their link with Confluent Education, but the *forms* of their development are very special and quite beyond the "classroom-bound," personal growth approaches of Confluent Education.

As mentioned above, in the case of Pacifica, Jung, rather than Freud or Perls, is the intellectual and spiritual godfather, and Aizenstat was strongly reinforced in this depth psychology orientation by James Hillman and the latter's Archetypal Psychology.

Finally, I see Aizenstat and Ferguson as *visionary leaders*, both somewhat tribal in orientation and both having left the stamp of their life experiences indelibly on these now thriving high-context institutions.

The Concord Institute

Current Description

The Concord Institute (Boston area) was founded in 1990 by Thomas R. Yoemans for the purpose of helping professionals who want to expand and deepen their work. In this institution, the programs and services teach professionals to include, and work responsibly and effectively with, the *spiritual dimension* of life, and to integrate it with the bio-psycho-social dimensions of human experience. While different programs respond to the needs of different professions, they are all intended to offer training for developing a *spiritual context* in professional work.

The Concord Institute is also part of an informal, international network of organizations and institutions that explore the spiritual aspects of counseling, psychotherapy, personal growth, and education. It offers programs in Spiritual Psychology, with monthly training seminars and weekly training groups, supplemented by reading, supervision, writing, and small group work.

The Institute's programs include Group Leadership (within a spiritual context), a Concord Institute Summer School for practitioners, and a referral network. In addition to Institute publications, there is a Global Psychology Project which focuses on the transcultural aspects of Spiritual Psychology, and an Eco-Psychology Project, exploring the correlation between ecological and spiritual responsibility.

The programs/services of the Concord Institute are designed for professionals who, whether psychologist, social worker, medical practitioner, clergy, teacher, counselor, or organizational consultant, want to be aware of, and work with several dimensions of human experience, particularly the spiritual dimension. They are intended to be tailored to the full-time professional, to those on sabbatical, or working part-time, and to graduate students who want to include them as part of their graduate studies. They are deemed most appropriate for those with previous training and experience in a professional discipline who want to make the commitment of time, energy, and resources to further intensive professional education. Preference is allegedly given to those with previous professional experience and/or an advanced professional degree (M.A., M.D., M.Div., M.S.W., Ph.D., R.N., or equivalent), or those working toward professional certification. Continuing Education Units are available for selected Institute programs.

The Story

In 1973, Thomas Yoemans received his Ph.D. degree in Confluent Education at UCSB and, therefore, I regard this Institute as very much a part of the institutional legacy of Confluent Education. His dissertation was entitled "Toward a Confluent Theory of Teaching English."

As the founder and director of the Concord Institute, Yoemans does the majority of the teaching and training, calling upon other qualified staff and guest teachers as needed. His background includes education at Harvard, Oxford, and the University of California, and professional work in the fields of literature, education, and psychology. Since 1970 he has worked as a therapist, teacher, and trainer of professionals in Psychosynthesis and, more recently, Spiritual Psychology, throughout North America and Europe. He has also taught in Russia and Lithuania. Since 1980 he has been interested as well in the issues of world order and planetary survival. This has led to a study of how the social problems of violence, hunger, pollution, and injustice correlate with the relative lack of psycho-spiritual maturity in the world today, and how these problems can be addressed from a spiritual perspective. He is also a published poet and writer, interested in the power of the creative arts as a means for the transformation of consciousness.

The main root of the Concord Institute has always been the doctrine and practice of Psychosynthesis, in which the founder, Thomas Yoemans, was formally trained in Italy and in the USA. Psychosynthesis was first formulated in 1910 by the Italian psychiatrist, Roberto Assagioli, and gradually developed over the last 85 years in Europe and North America.

Psychosynthesis draws on both Eastern and Western thought to describe how the spiritual self develops. Other subsidiary roots of the Concord Institute include Existentialism, Humanistic and Transpersonal Psychology, psychoanalysis, and the Native American culture. But, in my view, the most important recent development from the Concord Institute, far beyond a one-man operation, is the International School for Psychotherapy, Counseling and Group Leadership. This school opened in September 1995 and is the outcome of a five year joint effort of the "Harmony" Institute and the Transcultural Network for Global Psychology and Education.

The "Harmony" Institute for Psychotherapy and Counseling is espoused to be a pioneering, humanistically-oriented psychological treatment, training, and research center in St. Petersburg, Russia. Founded in July 1988, it was one of the first independent, non-governmental human service organizations in the former Soviet Union. It is allegedly highly respected throughout the former Soviet Union for its innovative role in the new Russian psychology. Also, it is currently one of the primary coordinating centers for hotline and emergency services, as well as practical training for psychotherapists and educators in Russia.

The Transcultural Network for Global Psychology and Education was founded in 1990 under the auspices of the Concord Institute in Concord,

MA, USA. Its members are mental health and education professionals from Northern America and Western Europe who are committed to transcultural and global work in their respective fields.

Since 1990 the Concord Institute and the Transcultural Network have provided comprehensive training in psychotherapy within a humanistic context at the "Harmony Institute". This work has led to the certification of the staff at "Harmony", publication of training materials in Russian, and the founding of the above mentioned International School for Psychotherapy, Counseling, and Group Leadership. As there appears to be a stark deficit of practical training in the formal Russian education system, with a complete absence of personal and experiential learning, this school is considered both unique and important in providing a different orientation to psychotherapy and group work.

The three year curriculum of the School is grounded in principles of Humanistic and Existential Psychology, as presented in the work of Carl Rogers, Carl Jung, Abraham Maslow, Roberto Assagioli, Victor Frankl, Fritz Perls, Rollo May, and others. The School's educational approach is based on the premise that a therapist, or a counselor, is the ultimate instrument of therapy and that in the course of professional training the process of personal and spiritual development is as important as extensive theoretical and technical education.

In contrast with the predominantly theoretical focus of traditional psychological training in Russia, the School gives priority to practical experience, thus broadening the horizon of the university education of its students. The primary mission of the International School is to prepare professionals for efficient practical work and this training process offers personal exploration and discovery as well as intellectual understanding and clinical skill.

The students of the School hopefully will work in the twenty-first century. With this in mind, this institution attempts to provide them with diverse crosscultural learning, synthesizing professional experience from different countries and a range of the psychological disciplines.

Link with Confluent Education

Even though Confluent Education per se is not mentioned in its brochures as one of the roots of the Concord Institute's philosophy, I do see a link between the former and the latter. As mentioned above,

Psychosynthesis has always been the main intellectual and spiritual root of the philosophy of the Concord Institute as stated by its founder and head, Thomas Yoemans in the foregoing "story" of the Institute.

Strangely, in my opinion, in one of the main current statements of Confluent Education, in the book *Advances in Confluent Education* (1996) the chapters by J. H. Brown (Introduction, p. xxvii) and models by Horowitz and J. H. Brown on Confluent evaluation research (p. 117) *do not* mention Yoeman's work in G. I. Brown's *The Live Classroom* (1975), pp. 80-90 and 132-158, nor his above mentioned doctoral dissertation (1973).

This is important in tracing the linkage between Confluent Education and the Concord Institute because Yoemans' model, along with the taxonomies of educational objectives by Benjamin Bloom and his colleagues (1964 and earlier) have been held forth by J. H. Brown and DeMuelle and Caston as "*the*" model of Confluent Education in *Advances in Confluent Education* (1996, pages referred to above).

In addition, DeMuelle and Caston, in the same 1996 work (*Advances in Confluent Education*), in their chapter on "A Coherent Vision of Teacher Education (pp. 43-62) also *never* mention Yoemans' model, although it is used extensively by them as a basic confluent model for bringing coherence to the sometimes intellectually chaotic field of teacher education. In fact, DeMuelle and Caston only peripherally refer to Bloom and his colleagues work once, in the following passage (as cited in *Advances in Confluent Education*, p. 44).

> During the 1960's, many educators began a re-exploration of teaching approaches to educate learners as whole human beings. This was done by addressing both cognition and affect, which includes values, emotions and personal beliefs, as an integral part of learning. (Krathwohl, Bloom, & Masia, 1964; Rogers, 1983; Satir, 1972)
>
> The early roots of Confluent Education were grounded in this movement (Brown, 1972, 1979; Brown, Phillips, & Shapiro, 1976).

Apparently the "advances" noted here in Confluent Education are based on the combination of Yoemans' and Bloom's models. This kind of Confluent model, however, has also become basic to the current professional legacy of Confluent Education as judged by the logo of the Confluent Education Newsletter (1996-1997), which is produced by the AERA Special Interest Group in Confluent Education and the overlapping core group of the professional Association of Confluent Educators.

In further examining the link between Confluent Education and the Concord Institute, Psychosynthesis continues to be a key issue. In the Confluent Education Program at UCSB Psychosynthesis was taught for a few years as an adjunct to Gestalt approaches to personal and professional development.

Psychosynthesis, however, in the Concord Institute, has increasingly led to a fully spiritual emphasis, as described in statements of current description and the "story" of the Institute's development.

In my opinion, there was and is a basic split between the philosophical and spiritual foundations of Psychosynthesis and Confluent Education. This was manifested, I think, by the essentially secular nature of Confluent Education and the limits of advocating a spiritual (religious?) doctrine at the public University of California. One could teach and inform *about* religions, but not practice or advocate them in the classrooms as part of the *public* domain.

Despite these bureaucratic, administrative constraints, I think there probably was some transpersonal awareness in Confluent Education as demonstrated by measures on the OTL and TOTL (see Chapter 1) and Shapiro and Fitzgerald (1989). In these studies of *humanistic* educators' instructional values, a transpersonal/spiritual dimension was discovered and, indeed, emerged as a paradigmatic factor in multivariate studies of authors' work and students' interests alike (see Table 1.1, Chapter 1).

However, considering the foregoing issues, I do *not* see a direct pattern of influence from Yeomans' experience in Confluent Education to the Concord Institute. The latter has moved in its own unique direction as have all of the exemplars of the institutional legacy of Confluent Education.

Interpretation

Like the other two leading figures studied here, I see Thomas Yoemans as a visionary leader. I consider him as a *"spiritual visionary,"* with a strong international orientation (e.g., The Transcultural Network for Global Psychology and Education, founded in 1990 under the auspices of the Concord Institute—headed by Yoemans as well as the development of the "Harmony Institute").

Like Stephen Aizenstat's Pacifica Graduate Institute, the Concord

Institute was founded relatively recently (1990 for the latter, and 1988 for the former). All three of the leaders studied in this section, but especially Aizenstat and Yoemans, were no longer young men in their 20s and all were experienced professionals for years before founding their respective institutions. Strictly speaking, however, Ferguson didn't found Santa Barbara Middle School but took over early in its history.

Like the first two institutions observed, the Concord Institute had a unique path of development and evolved into a particular form, far different and, in my opinion, beyond the Confluent Education Program at UCSB.

All of these institutions were originally energized and informed by significant humanistic doctrine despite their differences. And, in each case, the personal and professional lives of their leaders' were determining influences in the *way* these institutions developed and the differentiated forms they have taken. In each case, in my view, there was crucial influence by "gurus" or doctrines from "gurus," though this is not so obvious in Kent Ferguson's leadership at Santa Barbara Middle School. It is (to me) fascinating that the founder of Confluent Education, George Brown, apparently also had a conversion experience via Fritz Perls and Gestalt Therapy.

In many ways the three institutions reviewed here resembled the Confluent Education Program. The central similarity, in my opinion, being the underlying attempt to build a high-context, person-centered subculture—deliberately different from the traditional institutions which were prevalent at the time.

All, in my view, were expressions of the powerful Human Potential Movement which was sweeping important regions of our country and to some extent the Western World in the 1960s and 1970s. And in all cases, these institutions received significant emotional, intellectual and (sub-rosa) spiritual support and energy from Confluent Education—especially in the early stages of their ontology. I think this was largely due to the receptiveness of the charismatic visionaries, whose later missions energized the many loyal and competent followers necessary for the founding and survival of these highly innovative institutions.

Eventually Confluent Education did not survive academia. But none of the four legacy-institutions are in traditional academia and, to a large extent, I think that is one significant reason why they all have survived and are currently flourishing.

The Meta-senter for Confluent Education, Gestalt Therapy, and Psychosynthesis

Current Description

The Meta-senter is a private center for Confluent Education, Gestalt Therapy, and Psychosynthesis, founded in 1986 by the late Nils Magnar Grendstad, Ph.D. (1930-1993). Currently, the senter is directed by Liv Grendstad Rousseau, and provides training, consultation, and supervision to organizations, groups, and individuals interested in using Confluent Education, Gestalt, and Psychosynthesis principles. The senter has international contacts in Europe and North America, as well as in countries "east of the Baltic Sea." It is also a member of the Association for the Advancement of Psychosynthesis and The Transcultural Network.

At the heart of the Meta-senter's activities is a series of week-long training programs. The courses are organized for professionals with leadership supervision or teaching responsibilities.

The program is organized in 10 week-long courses or "steps." In these steps, principles of Confluent Education, Gestalt Therapy, and Psychosynthesis are integrated and presented to the students theoretically and experientially. The courses are designed around experiential learning (to learn is to discover) and provide the participants extensive practical training with various methods and techniques under the supervision of trainers. This experiential focus is utilized while maintaining the theoretical foundation, for the methods must also be well understood. Each step is organized so that after that step, the participant may practice what he/she has learned in everyday life and work life.

The program is organized into a series of 10 steps divided into three phases. The first 5 steps make up the first phase of the program. This phase provides a thorough introduction into simple, but effective methods, for use in one's personal and professional development as well as in the personal and professional supervision of others. The second phase is made up of steps 6, 7, and 8, which, using the same methods, provides a deeper and broader experience of Confluent Education, Gestalt Therapy, and Psychosynthesis principles. Phase Three, made up of steps 9 and 10, provides participants with a more specialized application of these principles in work with groups and organizations. Between each step, beginning with the first, participants are given "homework" which they are required to complete before going on to the next step. Each phase of the program finishes with a written paper which must be approved by the leader of the course and read and accepted by an external consultant. These papers include all material presented in each step, as well as in selected literature for the program.

The senter takes advantage of its international contacts by inviting experienced guest trainers to augment the depth and breadth of the training programs.

The Story

Actually, the story of this senter begins long before 1986. Nils Magnar Grendstad was born in 1930 on a small island near Trondheim in northern Norway. His father was "the teacher" on that island and Nils strongly identified with him and became a school psychologist, before meeting George Brown in Norway. Nils then became very involved with Confluent Education and Gestalt Therapy and completed a Ph.D. in Confluent Education at UCSB in 1975.

His dissertation topic on mental image perception revealed the influence of his Confluent training, combined with his long-term interests in schools, teacher-training, and teacher and student classroom behavior.

In my opinion, Nils' vision was to become a kind of missionary, taking his learning in Gestalt, Confluent Education, and later Psychosynthesis, and applying it to people who either couldn't afford these consciousness-raising methods or those professionals (especially in the health care field), who otherwise probably would not have had exposure to them.

After his Ph.D. in 1975, for a number of years he was employed in the Norwegian Teaching Academy in the College of Education and Theology as an instructor. However, apparently he felt that in that setting he could not fully transmit his core message of consciousness raising. He then began to search for other forms and roles, and that led to his vision of a private (proprietary) institution with only indirect connections with academia in Norway and the United States.

Most of the Meta-senter's programs have serviced schools of nursing throughout Norway. Later, the programs were so successful that the center included physicians, teachers and, to an impressive extent, even the military.

In accordance with his visionary calling, Nils, along with Tom Yoemans, took the center programs to Russia and Lithuania. In those countries, where he received no financial compensation, he served psychologists and physicians who, like the many nursing college people in Norway, could extend this orientation to their students, clients, and patients.

Since Dr. Grendstad's death in 1993, his daughter, Liv Grendstad Rousseau, who was part of the program, almost from its formal beginning in 1986, has acted as director and continues to head this flourishing, still innovative institution.

Liv Grendstad trained primarily by her father, after teacher-training at the University of Oslo, has taken Gestalt and Confluent methods to a somewhat different clientele—physiotherapists, seeking personal and professional growth and needing support groups in this often highly stressful profession. She now integrates the Meta-senter programs with the Norwegian Organization for Physiotherapists. The emphasis is on training counselors in Confluent Education and Gestalt methods as well as in small-group development.

Thus, some of the original orientation of the center has been applied to new settings. Liv Grendstad Rousseau, along with her small staff, now emphasize ethical issues and general reflection on professional practice.

Link with Confluent Education

Of all of the institutions surveyed in this section, the most direct link with Confluent Education and Gestalt therapy is in the Norwegian Meta-senter. Not only is this reflected in the name of the senter, but also in the philosophy and methods of training.

George and Judith Brown and Thomas Yoemans act as adjunct staff of the center. The former give advanced workshops in Gestalt methods and supervise the participants, and the latter trains people in Psychosynthesis.

In summary, both in methods and orientation, the link with Confluent Education here is the most specific and direct, as mentioned above. Also, I have trained people and observed others train participants in what could only be called small "c" confluent techniques. In addition, five to ten participants were students in various other confluent programs conducted by the Browns in the UCSB Confluent Education Program.

Interpretation

In a recent conversation with the current director of the program, I learned that her father, Nils Grendstad, thought that the three main components, Confluent Education, Gestalt, and Psychosynthesis, "all fit together." However, apparently Nils felt that while Confluent Education and Gestalt Therapy were the base, Psychosynthesis was *essential* in order to provide perspective.

In closing this section, I regard Nils Magnar Grendstad as an "international visionary"—a visionary leader with most of his graduate training in America, who saw and met a strong need in Norway and some eastern European nations. I also see him with much missionary zeal and applying it somewhat differently than the leaders in the other institutions in question. Nevertheless, the underlying similarities of all four institutional founders/leaders is most impressive, and will be further outlined in the following conclusions on the institutional legacy of Confluent Education.

Summary and Conclusions of the
Institutional Legacy of Confluent Education

Despite the similarities and connections (observed above) of Confluent Education with the institutional legacies studied here, it is my view that most of the impact of the former on the latter was *initially* generative in nature. This was because nearly all of the institutions studied became functionally autonomous from their Confluent origins in academia. They all took their own particular paths, as did the Confluent Education Program at UCSB. Yet, all five programs (institutions) were far more similar than different.

Only one of these institutions retained a *specifically* Confluent approach. The Meta-senter always did and still does use many characteristic Gestalt methods as integral to their programs, curricular, or extracurricular activities, in harmony with Gestalt as the mainstay ("backbone" of the Confluent Education Program at UCSB. See

Preface).

It is my view that, in the long run, the deepest influence Confluent Education has had is *at least* shared by the Human Potential Movement itself. Following the major premise of this book, Confluent Education was always so deeply embedded in the Human Potential Movement that parceling out the separate effects is ultimately problematic.

It wasn't the specific form of Confluent Education at UCSB which nourished and transferred to most of these "latter day" institutions and programs; rather, the fact that Confluent Education existed at all in the academy was foundational. Confluent Education was, like many other forms of Humanistic Education, all very much a part of the much broader Human Potential Movement. In my opinion, it didn't matter so much what the specific approach was named or even what it accomplished. What mattered most was that there was an active, academically and professionally legitimate humanistic educational form which trained people like Joel Brown, Marianne Caston, Sarah Jacobs, Margot Kenley, Stephen Aizenstat, Gary Linker, Nils Grendstad, and Thomas Yoemans, and many others.

We (in Confluent Education) launched these people and then they took off in their varied and creative ways and forms. Functional autonomy took over and each of the institutions observed generated its own unique style after the initial and significant "push" by their earlier developmental experiences at UCSB. They now make their contributions distinctly and distinctively.

My interpretation of Confluent Education's institutional legacy includes deep respect for its generative power. But this history has again shown me how many creative and effective educational forms the "Humanist Impulse" can take, with or without the specific features of Confluent Education. While more general approaches like programs which aim to develop self-esteem, cooperative learning, group process, body and spiritual awareness have applied distinctive methods, they were all in the spirit of the Human Potential Movement (see OTL studies, Chapter 1 on the instructional values of humanistic educators).

Confluent Education legitimized and prepared the humanistic leaders/educators who entered its programs for their future roles, and some became founders and leaders of their own institutions. Each had his or her own vision of what a learning and growth-oriented institution might become. So, as a primarily germinal influence, Confluent Education leaves a rich institutional legacy.

Table 4.1 summarizes what I think of as significant characteristics of the institutional leaders examined above. With the possible exception of Kent Ferguson, who at age 32, inherited the Santa Barbara Middle School from Margot Kenley, the founders/leaders were experienced, middle-aged white men, mostly in their 40s, and one in his 50s (average age 46+ years).

Table 4.1 indicates (by a √ in a circle) what I believe to be these leaders/founders' primary role to be. In all cases, however, it includes several checks for each leader. All were "visionary leaders" in my opinion, but their *primary* visionary roles were as follows:

George Brown:	Gestalt Education visionary
Kent Ferguson:	Tribal visionary
Stephen Aizenstat:	Entrepreneurial-Depth Psychology visionary
Thomas Yoemans:	Spiritual visionary
Nils Grendstad	International visionary

These variations in primary role are, perhaps, actually secondary to their being visionary leaders who have had more than one original emphasis. For example, all but George Brown, the "father figure" in Confluent Education, were spiritually-oriented visionaries, as indicated in their current programs. This, I find significant evidence (if the labels are valid) of the functional autonomy of each institution but, at the same time, confirming the importance of a transpersonal orientation in Humanistic Education, which I documented with Louise Fitzgerald in our observations and construction of the "Transpersonal Orientation to Learning" scales (TOTL) (Shapiro & Fitzgerald, 1989).

The remainder of the visionary leadership classifications appear well-distributed throughout the rest of the four categories in Table 4.1. Further, I perceived only one significant Gestalt Education orientation (Grendstad) apart from the founder of Confluent Education himself, George Brown. This again (to me) reveals the variation underlying the most important generalization about these leaders; namely, that they were all leaders with a vision and, indeed, a mission which they fulfilled in a significant way. They were outstanding in Humanistic Education within the Human Potential Movement.

I did not include here many others mentioned in this book, who also made important contributions to Affective, Psychological, or Humanistic Education simply because they were not leaders in the institutions chosen as examples of primary legacies of Confluent Education.

Table 4.1

Visionary Leaders

Age	Institution	Founder/ Leader	Year	Gestalt education	Tribal	Entrepreneurial/ depth psychology	Spiritual	Inter- national	God-father/ God-mother
43	UCSB — Confluent Education	George Brown	1966	⊘				✓	Frederick Perls
32	Santa Barbara Middle Schol	Kent Ferguson	1976		⊘		✓		Margot Kenley
40	Pacifica Graduate Institute	Stephen Aizenstat	1989		✓	⊘	✓		Carl Jung, J. Hillman
46	Concord Institute	Thomas Yoemans	1990				⊘	✓	Roberto Assagioli
56	Meta-senter	Nils Grendstad	1986	✓			✓	⊘	George Brown, Frederick Perls, Roberto Assagioli

LEGEND:

⊘ = Primary Orientation

In addition to the common and varied visionary role of these leaders shown in Table 4.1, I saw other significant commonalities, including:

1. All are "lofty" and somewhat grandiose in their pronouncement, claims, ambitions, etc. Furthermore, most of these claims are not usually supported by empirical evidence other than their professional, legitimized existence, certification, etc. This feature of grandiosity apparently "comes with the territory" of visionaries.

2. All were/are more or less (mostly "more") entrepreneurial. All of the institutions, including Confluent Education at UCSB, were/had to be "businesses" in order to survive.

3. All had conversion reactions to one or more gurus who became the "Godfathers/Godmothers" of their institutions and their work.

4. All had important links to Confluent Education, but varied in the direct influence of Confluent Education in their current programs. But in the process, they built and retained their unique identities as separate from the original Confluent Education Program.

5. All are high-context subcultures, and none are subordinate or closely tied to external academic institutions. They are all free-standing, private educational enterprises.

6. In spite of the above, in my perspective, all these legacy institutions, in their entirety, tend to validate Confluent Education as a vital, needed, and creative program which met its demise in 1993 basically because it was founded and functioning within the restraints of the academy. Attempting to build a high-context subculture surrounded by powerful low-context forms and forces eventually overcame Confluent Education. Partly because the other four examples of the institutional legacy of Confluent Education were "free standing" schools, they still survive and flourish.

Professional Legacy

The New Generation

In the introduction to this chapter, I mentioned the difficulties inherent in tracking the legacies of Confluent Education, be they institutional, professional, or cultural. "Blending," being one of the root meanings of Confluent Education, also suggests that it might be problematic to *separate* the various influences on the professional legacy of Confluent Education.

This is so not only because the various legacies "blend" together, making them difficult to analyze and to differentiate them from one another, and also hard to distinguish them from other broad influences. For example, is the Norwegian Meta-senter primarily an institutional or a professional legacy of Confluent Education?

Although I did offer the Meta-senter as a prime example of the institutional legacy of Confluent Education, it could also be thought of as a *professional legacy* because the training in this center is oriented toward instructional professionals who transfer much of the philosophy and methods of Confluent Education and Gestalt to professional schools of nursing, medicine, education, physiotherapy, the military etc. In addition, I find the cultural legacy even more diffuse and almost impossible to separate from other sources.

It could be argued, however, that parceling out the effects, and analyzing these legacies is contrary to "wholeness" principles so prominent in most humanistic philosophies. Also acknowledging the many interactive sources makes an understanding of the various effects of Confluent Education more obscure and, at some point, quite beyond the scope of this book.

With the above caveat in mind, I have chosen to illustrate the generational changes in the leadership of Confluent Education as evidenced by several of the new (1996) books interpreted in Chapter 3. But the most visible professional effects to me are the development of the research-oriented AERA Special Interest Group ("SIG") in Confluent Education, and the newly formed practitioner-oriented Association of Confluent Educators (ACE). Next I will look to identified, confluently-oriented elementary school teachers and administrators for examples of current professional practice. These education professionals were all trained through UCSB, either in Teacher Education or Educational Administration or both.

The Current Confluent Education Professional Group

Typical of my sources on Confluent professionals will be from several issues of the Confluent Education Newsletters, March 1996 and June 1997.

In the March 1996 issue, a conference was reported to have been held in Southern California with the "concept": "To keep the actions of Confluent Education Alive." This was a continuation of previous, similar conferences and it was decided by the participants to hold regional meetings for local groups. These groups were to form local Confluent chapters, including Northern and Southern California, the Southeast U.S., Canada, Europe, and the U.S. East Coast.

This included locating new sources of funding for existing Confluent research, and "most importantly" finding ways to engage *all* members in the SIG functions. This was to *reestablish* a strong community spirit where "everyone has a place" and hopefully encourage more people to become involved.

This issue of the Newsletter also proposed more specific future directions for Confluent Education, especially the broad-based "Association of Confluent Educators" (ACE), which emphasizes professional concerns. The following expressed the "vision" of the conference:

> Our vision is to create a center for Confluent Education with non-profit status. It will be governed by a board of directors that is comprised of the president or representative of each local chapter and the AERA SIG, the coordinator of on-going Confluent Education projects, and someone with fund-raising expertise.

The June 1997 issue of the Confluent Newsletter includes a message from the incoming chair (of the AERA Confluent Education SIG), Joel Brown, in which he asserted: "American education is in the midst of its first reformation in over 100 years, which during the same period, technology has often moved faster than our collective wisdom has comprehended."

He further noted: "Ironically, given our extensive confluent educational knowledge concerning communication, perhaps we have not taken advantage of the technological revolution. . . ."

Brown's espoused intention is to encourage national and international communication and he proposed:
1. Creating a Confluent Education web site.
2. Creating a Confluent Education "list serve."
3. Visiting each national and international region.
4. Increasing the membership and participation levels.
5. Raising funds for research and programs.

A complex chart of the Association for Confluent Education (ACE) was also presented in this issue of the Newsletter, connecting the numerous widespread SIG chapters with ACE but apparently subsuming the SIG group *under* the now-broadened umbrella of the ACE. Upcoming tasks in research, professional development, and structural operations were also included in what appears to me to be a very ambitious enterprise.

My interpretation of these pieces from two typical Confluent newsletters is that this does represent, in theory and intention, at least, a very vigorous and ambitious set of plans to organize and greatly expand Confluent Education, in order to revive it after its academic demise at UCSB in 1993. As mentioned above, it also represents a generational shift in leadership, with the exception of Judith Brown.

As such, this does represent a *valid professional legacy* of the Confluent Education Program at UCSB. Whether these plans can be implemented remains to be seen, because of the ambitiousness and proliferation of professional subgroups, charters, etc. in such a relatively few years (1993-97). I see it as an attempt at full revival and expansion of Confluent Education without an institutionalized, academic base.

I think that this could be a difficult program to sustain, despite the obvious energy and involvement of a new generation of Confluent Educators.

Professional Legacy in the Local Schools

Locating and contacting confluently-oriented teachers and administrators in the local schools (Santa Barbara area) proved to be much more difficult than I had expected. Apparently, only a handful of active professionals identify themselves as "Confluent people."

Through seven sources for finding such people in school systems with well over 1,000 professionals, I found approximately five or six of them. My sources came from secondary and elementary schools in the Santa Barbara and Goleta School Districts, and some from the Teacher Education Program at UCSB, and some references were supplied by veteran principals or central office personnel.

Most of the people identified were in their 40s or 50s and several recently retired. My sources from the "new generation" Confluent revival professional groups also reported that few teachers or administrators attended their meetings or retreats (perhaps 1 or 2 in an approximately 25-person group).

The entire local population informally surveyed for signs of a Confluent orientation to education included 910 secondary and elementary teachers and administrators from the Santa Barbara School District, and 257 from the Goleta Elementary School District. The total was 1,117 professionals. Thus, the six administrators and teachers who were clearly identified by general personal/professional validation as having a Confluent orientation represented only a fraction of 1% of the professionals allegedly included in this limited and informal survey. Even if at least 10 clearly "Confluent people" were located, that would still represent a tiny fraction (less than 1 in 100) of professionals in these school districts.

A note from one of my most knowledgeable sources in Teacher Education at UCSB indicated that "there really aren't Confluent Education people out there in the Santa Barbara schools." She also observed that most folks in their later years went into leadership or research positions. With difficulty and some delay, she identified a few people who might be considered as having a Confluent orientation. Compare this with 529 (Santa Barbara County) teachers out of a total 3,200 teachers in the county (16%+) who applied for Impact II, The Teachers Network which includes *all* school personnel in a current collaborative effort to improve the quality of education in this area ("Reaching New Heights," 1997, p. 48).

Several case studies are offered as examples of current professionals in the local schools who could be considered to embody a professional legacy from Confluent Education. As far as I know, none of them have had Confluent training or retraining in the past 15 years.

Local "Confluent" School Teachers and Administrators

Example 1

LM, age 43 years, Vice-Principal of a local elementary K-6, Charter School was referred to me by the supervisor of bilingual training in the Teacher Education Program at UCSB's Graduate School of Education. According to this supervisor, who knew and trained many teachers in the local schools, LM came to mind first when I asked who had a primarily "Confluent orientation" in the local public schools. My 1 1/2 hour interview with LM was part of my investigation of the professional legacy of Confluent Education in the schools.

As I approached the somewhat old fashioned elementary school, built in 1929, I noticed a group of teachers (presumably) having an informal conference at the entrance to a small windowless office just off the main hall. I was directed back to this corner by the main office person, and there I met LM, still conferring with the teachers on "V," a non-English speaking, Latino boy. The group was led by what turned out to be LM, on the family and learning dynamics, regarding what they called a second language issue. LM was talking about her "gut level feeling" about "V" and his culture and the family influence. As I waited for LM to complete her conference, I noticed young, apparently vigorous teachers, moving in what seemed to be a friendly, informal, connective atmosphere, where cookies were just being served at 10:00 a.m., my appointment time for LM. I waited for approximately 10-15 minutes and chatted with various staff people and teachers. Again I introduced myself and entered LM's office.

I asked LM to begin by telling her "story"—both personal and professional. She began with a metaphor for her life—a very special walkway at UCSB (to her), which she constantly revisits and often visualizes.

She was reared in Orange County, CA in an Italian Catholic family in a very WASP neighborhood in which she never felt very comfortable—as though she didn't quite belong there—green-eyed and blonde-haired—though she was and is, she identified herself as "Latina" and that identity crystallized for her when she entered UCSB at age 18 years.

At that point, about 15-20 minutes into the interview, we were interrupted. The door was not completely closed on purpose because LM had advised the office staff of her interview with me (for privacy), but that she was available if needed.

A teacher of kindergarten brought 5-year-old (in August 1997) "Juan," into the windowless, warm, almost hot 11" x 11" office for "discipline," since that was acknowledged as one of LM's duties as Vice-Principal. It seemed that Juan was stealing from other children's' lunches and did not obey the teacher's orders to stop that behavior.

For about 5 minutes, Juan sat silently, His shoes did not come close to touching the floor, in that "adult chair" in the corner of her office. LM continued her interview with me.

After a short interval, she turned to the child and began speaking to him in apparently fluent Spanish in a soft but distinct way, asking him questions but not getting much response. She then suggested that he draw something which interested him or showed what he was feeling, and she took one of my pens, gave it to him, and he immediately and vigorously began his "picture." LM told Juan that the purpose of the drawing was to let his *teacher know* how he was feeling *and* how he thought he could behave with his teacher. I heard the instructions as gentle and yet firm and from Juan's response, I surmise that she had "gotten through" to him very effectively.

When Juan quickly finished his drawing, LM again turned to him and interviewed him in Spanish on his drawing. She praised his drawing, calling it "excellente," as she moved her chair closer to him and in a soothing, rhythmical voice, asked him what the picture meant. He responded in soft, "little boy" Spanish, contrasted with almost no verbal response previously, as he continued to play with my pen. (Was it really mine?)

Now she whispered to him, pointed to him, then at his drawing, and gently touched his chest as she asked him to sign his name at the bottom of the picture. She again says "excellente" as he signed his name, and she asked to whom would he give the picture. He responded quickly and said he would give it to his "Mommie and Poppie."

She asked again what the picture was and he quickly replied, "water." Then she asked, "What do you do with 'water'?" and he said, "I swim." He said he likes to swim, and then LM asked him who takes care of him when he swims so that he's okay in the water and who tells him to get out of the water when it's time to do that? and he replied, "Mommie."

Then LM asked Juan, "Who is this picture for?" When he again said, "Mommie," LM asked is it for *other people* who take care of you when you swim?" and he said "Yes." Responding to Juan's last "yes," she then asked, who are these people, other than his mother? He responded by saying it is also his father, brother, and sister.

Then LM asked Juan, "Who in your classroom takes care of you?" But Juan didn't respond (probably because, not having had any pre-schooling, he didn't have a concept of the role of the "maestra" [teacher]).

At that point, Juan acknowledged his classroom teacher as one who takes care of him, and when asked what he will now say to his teacher, he responded by saying he will tell his teacher that he was "sorry" for what he did ("lo siento").

LM then said to Juan in Spanish, "I'm *so* glad, because your teacher was feeling *sad* that you weren't listening to her."

Before escorting Juan back to his teacher and classroom, LM took his hand and used each of her fingers to identify the people who take care of him—mother, father, brother, and sister—and *pointed out his thumb* as representing his teacher. She then rehearsed this symbol by going through it with him also using her own hand to duplicate it and touched each of her fingers and then his corresponding digits.

She then left the office with Juan, for about 5-10 minutes, and then returned to the interview situation. I asked her to describe what I saw and what she did, and she called it "Integrative Learning," because if she can, she uses *any* resource or modality, or event to facilitate learning from the student's point of view.

This was (to me) an inspiring and (to her) a totally spontaneous example of her professional role as a gentle authority, a healer, and connector of this child to himself, his family and his culture, the teacher, to the classroom, and to the school. Apparently, this is an environment in which he has felt quite uncomfortable.

To my questions searching for more specific or formal links with Confluent Education, she replied that her "natural" approach to teaching and collaborating with others was to some degree reinforced by a "Confluent" teacher-supervisor at UCSB—mainly that it was "okay to be a teacher like she was naturally."

LM apparently did not and does not remember or use most of the specific group process techniques she had in teacher education or any other "Confluent" techniques. What she does remember, she derived from her experience as a Cooperative Learning peer coach and the seminars in the Cooperative Learning Institute.

My impression of this particular example of the professional legacy of Confluent Education suggests that for LM, at least, this represented only an indirect professional legacy from Confluent Education per se and that given LM's strong humanistic/nurturing orientation, she would have taken a very similar professional path with or without Confluent Education.

I find Confluent Education playing a supportive, but subordinate, role in LM's personal and professional development. Her orientation involves the spontaneous and (I think) very creative/integrative use of an impressive "bag of tools," derived from her own life experiences and her extensive professional training and experience. Using "orientation," "techniques," and "personal validation" as criteria for a Confluent professional legacy, I found only her personal and professional validation as a completely fulfilled criterion.

Example 2

SW is beginning her seventh year as an elementary school principal, having had 21 years experience as an elementary teacher, mostly in the local schools.

She has had much exposure to Confluent training and retreats and was a guest member (as the wife of a DRICE teacher) of DRICE for several years. However, she has not had formal, academic training in Confluent Education.

SW still considered herself a "Confluent Educator" even though she does not attend the current "renewal groups" described in the previous section of this chapter.

She reported that she "saw a lot of nice strategies" within the DRICE program which helped her make more direct contact with people on sensitive issues and find non-threatening ways to help them address personal feelings when they felt safe and ready to do that. This orientation to her work as a principal was also largely true in her role as a teacher.

Apparently she sees her role in disciplinary situations as more of a facilitator than an authority, laying down the law. She alleges that she brings children, teachers, staff, and parents to a small round table in her room and tries to help people solve problems with one another or the school by dealing honestly with feelings, using "I statements" and encouraging eye contact among the people involved.

Of particular concern to SW was to show children their own responsibility for much of what happens—especially in interpersonal conflicts and relationships, but claimed she was very aware of "age-appropriate" methods for doing this.

She reported that she regarded her Confluent training as instrumental in her role in these kinds of situations. According to her, it gave her more skills and confidence in using such techniques as guided imagery, simulation exercises, and especially in improving her listening skills, with children, staff, and parents.

It appeared especially important to SW that the powerful methods of Confluent Education not be used coercively. She did see some coercion in a few cases and she deeply resented this manipulation—especially of children. This temporarily dampened her allegiance to Confluent Education, but on subsequent reflection, it was remembered as a vital learning experience for her.

Also, SW values empowerment of children and others in constructive ways, and she was particularly appreciative of her own empowerment and self-confidence as a result of her work in Confluent Education and with UCSB professor Homer Swander, in the role-playing exercises he conducted in his Shakespeare classes.

SW has also recently completed a Ph.D. in the Educational Leadership and Organization Program in UCSB's Department of Education, and has been active in promoting the use of technology in the classroom, in adult education. In addition, she has been trained and taught in the South Coast Writing Program at UCSB.

She also noted that many of the people she knew in DRICE and Confluent Education have retired or taken other paths than her own. In her own case, however, Confluent Education appears to have had a direct, important influence in her personal and professional life. For example, she sees herself as becoming more empathetic and reflective than simply reactive, especially in highly stressful situations.

In conclusion, SW felt that she was deeply validated by her Confluent experiences. To quote her, "I, and many others, found our voice, that it was OK to speak up—and many of us didn't know what our own voice was, especially the women."

At the end of the interview I mentioned to her the triad of orientation, techniques, and validation as interacting criteria for identifying a viable professional legacy from Confluent Education. In the case of SW, I perceive a strong professional legacy which was often manifested in her general professional orientation, the preferred techniques she used in her role as a teacher and an administrator, and especially in a strong sense of personal and professional validation.

She did state, however, that most of her staff were *not* confluently oriented. Apparently her orientation did not specifically translate to most of her staff, except insofar as probably she is and has been an important role model for other professionals with whom she has interacted in her long service to education.

Example 3

SP is a 58-year-old local elementary school teacher with 29 years experience—25 years in the local schools. She was relatively young-sounding and appearing woman who has specialized in English, speech arts, and drama—mostly in the upper elementary school (fifth and sixth grades).

SP alleged that her major orientation to teaching is being a *humanist* with the children, which to her meant being respectful of them and, when appropriate, treating them like peers, in and out of the classroom.

Her professional training in the 1970s involved work in the National Endowment for the Humanities LIT Project, in which she studied literature (mostly classics) in depth and how to teach children ways of reading and writing using the classics. She was also trained and taught at UCSB in the South Coast Writing Project, and she has done extensive consulting for them "all over" the State of California.

SP has had no formal training in Confluent Education but she has been supported by principals with what she regards as a unique philosophy of education, leading to the open classroom, multi-level teaching and, ultimately, a humanistic/confluent approach. One of her schools was in the DRICE project, centered at UCSB.

In that project she remembered many brainstorming sessions with her principal and other teachers on how to be "humanistic" with children. She has always had what she calls a child-centered, person-centered approach very compatible with a specifically Confluent orientation. Her primary approach to teaching appears to be broadly humanistic and confluent (with a lower case "c"). She observes:

> Our school became a space—a sanctuary of safety, trust, and love. We (teachers) respected one another and the children, almost as colleagues. Before my contact with Confluent Education I did not have a model of teaching other than my own intuition, on which I've always relied. But a model was very helpful.
>
> I also did a lot of "values education" and looked on my classroom as a special community, with a particular culture. This involved valuing everyone's personal beliefs, even if they were different from your own.

SP also noted that Confluent Education gave her permission to "bring all the children on board" and valued crosscultural diversity.

Apparently, this constituted significant personal and professional validation for the kind of person and kind of teacher she already was.

In terms of techniques, she reported:

> Whatever I learned was through in-service training, lots of group process skills and experience in empathetic listening. I also learned to participate with the children. I share what I write with them. I do every assignment I give them. I ask them for feedback, critique, questions, revisions, etc. In that way, I model how difficult good writing can be.
>
> Through this training and experience and with great support from my principals, I feel I grew tremendously. I found what people called "flair" in my work. For example, we had an open classroom which was turned into a Shakespearean Theater. There were no doors between the three rooms. There were three teachers and a mixture of children from high-third grade, and fourth, fifth, and sixth grade. It involved lots of work in scheduling and regrouping, but it was great!

In my view, SP meets all three criteria of general orientation, techniques, and validation for a humanistic educator—not formally Confluent—but deeply influenced by it because it was available to her as an opportunity for growth and gave needed structure to her work.

Finally, SP remarked about other teachers who were oriented in a broadly humanistic way in the local elementary schools, but felt that very few would now identify themselves as "Confluent teachers." According to her, the term "Confluent" is rarely, if ever, used at the present time.

Example 4

RW is a 49-year-old local elementary school teacher who describes his current general orientation to teaching as "extremely eclectic." He stated:

> I do what works. It's no one thing, but my philosophy is "humanist." I have specialized over time, like many other teachers I know. It's different from the 70s when I did have some contact with Confluent educators, near the end of the DRICE program. We had sensitivity then. I work a lot harder but it's much more organized and structured than at that earlier time. We had great process through Confluent Education, but *no substance*. I have both now.

He reported that he completed elementary teacher training at UCSB in 1972, but that:

> The University was very lacking then in connecting with me and my needs and I guess Confluent Education especially modified my principal which made up for that to a large extent. Now we have cooperative teaching and learning, but we have much more substance, like in new math and writing. We also have much more accountability now for what we do.
>
> In the 70s, DRICE did validate me and my teaching. It was a powerful source of energy, but the times themselves were pretty confusing. It also gave me tools to deal with the energy of groups of children or adults. "Confluent" gave me tools to do that and it helped my intuition. It gave me enough confidence to trust my intuition. "N," my principal, was very helpful. He filtered the Confluent stuff so it made more sense to me and fit the real world more.

He further stated that he recalled the author's presence at some of the in-service meetings with the teachers and the principal ("N"):

> With you there was no agenda other than how to deal with a powerful person like "N" and it was very appropriate for us at that time. But in time I felt there was no leader (principal or group leader) for me to depend on. I was ready to move on and become "my own guy."
>
> Now, all that stuff is woven into the curriculum. As in writing and sharing stories, collaboration in the new math, but I think the *passion* for teaching is missing now.
>
> I still use some Confluent stuff like Perls (Gestalt) things and group process skills, but we've learned a lot since then. I'm a lot more gentle now and we have a very different curriculum.
>
> I don't find many people nowadays who have that same depth of understanding of the kids and the curriculum with all its new demands, like multicultural, bilingual needs. Confluent Education is only a term for emphasizing process and a child-centered approach, but not at all like Summerhill where it was all blended together.

I found RW to be very much like the other three examples of the professional legacy of Confluent Education.

He is the same age group (near 50 years) and had much the same kind of exposure to Confluent Education in the early and mid-1970s via in-service training by myself and other Confluent educators. Also, his principal was an excellent model for a humanistically-oriented school, as well as providing something of a buffer between the less practical aspects of the Confluent approach and the pragmatic applications to the real world of children, teaching, and school.

However, RW had some reservations about Confluent Education (lacking in substance and structure) and he has apparently "become his own person." Like some of the other examples, he was significantly influenced by Confluent Education in his general orientation, of techniques, and personal and professional validation. Therefore, I regard him as another valid example of the professional Confluent legacy.

Summary of Professional Legacy in the Local (Public) Schools

In the above four examples, a kind of Confluent professional legacy in the local schools was amply demonstrated, in my opinion.

Even though LM was not considered a complete exemplar of Confluent Education, the orientations, techniques, and validation of all four mature, experienced administrators and teachers (average age 50 years) were far more alike than different. In each case, the respondent espoused the orientation and values of Humanistic Education in general and apparently Confluent Education made a significant contribution to that genre.

They used similar techniques and all experienced personal and professional validation of which they are clearly aware at the present time. The overlapping of their stories almost 25 years *after* their exposure to Confluent Education is striking and confirms a generalized, professional legacy in a small group of dedicated and effective teachers. This indicates to me that their work is *not* merely and *extension* of Confluent Education, but a genuine "inheritance" from the past—a still active, but diminishing professional legacy in the local public schools.

Apparently, in the local schools in the Santa Barbara area, there are a diminishing handful of Confluent teachers and administrators in the elementary schools. In the above four cases, none were fully trained in the Confluent Education degree programs at UCSB. They were, however, significantly influenced by participation in DRICE, Confluent Education retreats, and colleagues who did have formal training in Confluent Education.

Most of the active local professionals were in their 40s and 50s, but many have retired, changed their focus, or moved away, and many moved out of the teaching profession. Therefore, to consider a full professional legacy in the local schools is dubious in terms of significant numbers of teachers and administrators who are identifiable as Confluent Educators. Furthermore, in this group, I could not find any "Confluent School" in the institutional sense of a legacy.

The effects of the original exposure to Confluent Education now appears to be thoroughly diffused among many *other humanistic approaches* to education. Various new forms of curriculum (e.g., Cooperative Learning, whole language approaches to reading and writing, new interactive math, a multicultural emphasis, English as a Second Language, etc.) predominate the current curricula.

In my opinion, the above again illustrates the place of Confluent Education in a post-modern form of the Human Potential Movement. Still, we can speak of active "carriers" of the legacy—those relatively few individuals significantly affected by Confluent Education in the 1970s who have modified it to fit today's challenges in schools.

I do not include the apparently widespread organizational and professional consulting as a *legacy* of Confluent Education, but rather an extension of a part of this approach which has continued into the present. There is no denying, however, that Gestalt and other Confluent orientations have significantly influenced many current professionals in the organizational/institutional field (e.g., HRD positions in business and industry, and free lance management consultants to businesses and public institutions like community colleges and government agencies).

This distinction between "legacy" and "extension" could be regarded as splitting hairs and that could well be the case here. Suffice it to say, I have chosen here to exclude organizational consulting as a "legacy" in a strict sense of that term, but not because it isn't an important part of the work of today's Confluent educators (for example, see George Brown, Barott & Kleiveland, and Fernando Gapasin in the recent (1996) book edited by Joel Brown, *Advances in Confluent Education*).

Cultural Legacy

As mentioned in the introduction to this chapter, determining the cultural legacy of this program and its offshoots is difficult because cultural legacies are often from many intertwined sources. And that is the case in Confluent Education, if "legacy" is defined in nonlegalistic terms as "something coming from ancestors or predecessors—a situation which exists as a result of events and conditions, in the past." It is usually regarded as something passed on or left behind which remains after the source has passed on (e.g., The Joseph Campbell Archives at Pacifica Graduate Institute).

Thus, it is still very difficult (for me) to distinguish between a legacy from the past and merely a current form or continuation/extension of a program or movement which is still active (e.g., the theories and current applications of Confluent Education noted in *Advances in Confluent Education*, edited by Joel H. Brown and published in 1996).

I do not expect to find an identifiable, specific cultural legacy from Confluent Education in the arts, language, literature, music, or the disciplinary humanities. Any such effect, if any existed, would be hopelessly interwoven with all the other similar "humanistic" programs and movements listed in the introduction to this chapter. For example, Confluent Education never has had a long-term logo, clearly identified with the program. No songs, traditions, rituals, or artifacts remain, to my knowledge.

To narrow the field of cultural effects I will focus on a few more or less concrete examples of what I do regard as legitimate legacies in the cultural sense. These include the Archives of Humanistic Psychology in the UCSB Library, and the Campbell and Gimbutas collections and, finally, some observations on the general combined effects of post-modern thinking in history from the work of the noted historian Joyce Oldham Appleby. The latter, however, amply illustrates the diffusion of the effects of programs like Confluent Education in the whole Human Potential Movement, *which together* probably represent a kind of cultural legacy.

The UCSB Archives of Humanistic Psychology

The UCSB Archives of Humanistic Psychology were created in 1987 through the efforts of California State Assemblyman John Vasconcellos, who was mentioned in Chapter 1 as a powerful political ally of Confluent Education. John Vasconcellos became a close friend of George and Judith Brown through their work at the Esalen Institute in the late 1960s and until the mid-1970s.

Vasconcellos obtained a grant from the State of California for the establishment of these archives to be located on a UC campus. I think UCSB was chosen primarily because of the Browns-Vasconcellos connection and the singular nature of the Confluent Education Program in the university as a whole. Note that the scope of these archives is far greater than Confluent Education, but Confluent Education was the connecting link of an actual UC Program within the broader humanistic field.

One of the main purposes of these archives was to impact disciplines other than psychology, beyond psychotherapy, and including humanistic organizational development—a field which this Confluent Education Program strongly embraced at that time. So, the mission of the archives *was* cultural in effect, because outside of the Carl Rogers' collection elsewhere, there was no large depository for books, diaries, papers, journals, transcripts, tapes (video and audio), etc. in existence.

The archives serve many clients at this time as a very rich source of research and scholarly interest in the entire spectrum of humanistic endeavors. However, they do not function as a collection of the disciplinary humanities or even as a primarily link between human potential approaches to knowledge and experience and the classical disciplinary humanities.

To conclude this example, I am (almost) certain that the archives would not have been located at UCSB were it not for the strong personal and professional relationship between Vasconcellos and the Browns and, equally important, Vasconcellos' high regard for the Confluent Education Program at UCSB. He perceived it as the most humane and humanistic outpost in the UC system.

The Joseph Campbell and Marija Gimbutas Archives at Pacifica

These archives have been described in the section of this chapter on the institutional legacy of Confluent Education, but I do regard their presence at Pacifica, and the many scholarly uses to which they have been put, to be both a local and more universal cultural resource. This extensive collection of over 3,000 books, papers, etc. of Joseph Campbell are also central to the Doctoral Program in Mythology and Depth Psychology at Pacifica, but their influence is far broader than Pacifica and, therefore, I regard it as a cultural legacy of Confluent Education to the extent that Confluent Education was influential in the development of the founders of Pacifica, Stephen Aizenstat and Gary Linker. This connection is also noted in the section on the institutional legacy of Confluent Education.

I regard the Marija Gimbutas archives as a cultural legacy of Confluent Education in the same sense as the Campbell archives. As noted above, Gimbutas was a professor of neolithic archeology at UCLA and this also significantly expanded Pacifica's educational resources.

Together the placement of these archives at Pacifica could encourage other scholars to contribute their papers and effects to Pacifica, helping to make it an even more important cultural legacy in the sense as noted above.

Joyce Oldham Appleby

Eminent historian, Joyce Appleby, professor of history at UCLA, is currently president of the American Historical Association. In my opinion, the cultural legacy which she represents comes from many sources, a new generation of post-modern historians, especially since the 1960s, educationally-minded scholars from UCLA's National Center for History in the Schools, post-empirical history, the evolving philosophy of history, feminism, and constructivism.

She is offered as an example of many branches of social science, education, and philosophy coming together as a kind of cultural legacy. While Confluent Education is not identifiable as a source in this "mixture" of forces, it is certainly compatible with the more subjective, holistic, meanings-oriented ways of knowing which Appleby and an increasing number of other scholars appear to be embracing at this time.

Conclusions on Cultural Legacy

To me, the limitations in determining a cultural legacy of Confluent Education stand out in the brevity of the above discussion. Cultural artifacts, detectable influence in the arts and humanities are not to be found at this time. In a larger sense, however, broad movements which the historian Appleby studies, reinforce my notion that Confluent Education, along with many other reflections of humanism was and is embedded in the broad Human Potential Movement which, in turn, is embedded in what I have termed the "Humanist Impulse." Apparently, this force has recurred many times in human history, in both overt and covert forms.

Probably it is in the forms of amalgamated practices, instructional values, and curricula, in certain subcultures, where traces of a cultural legacy from Confluent Education might be detected. But, aside from concrete manifestations such as archives, etc. the pervasive diffusion of effects makes it very difficult and perhaps unwise to separate a particular Confluent cultural legacy from the broad legacy of the Human Potential Movement itself.

The Legacy of Confluent Education: Conclusions to Chapter 4

A legacy is defined here as institutions, professional activities, or cultural effects of Confluent Education. These are values and practices passed on through events which happened at an earlier time. There is usually a perceivable time gap between the original and its legacies.

It is now over 30 years since the inception of Confluent Education in 1966. It was founded by George Brown and his education colleagues at Esalen Institute, and I think of it as deeply embedded in the prevailing culture of Esalen and the Human Potential Movement.

The legacy of Confluent Education has been relatively difficult to identify because of the diffusion of effects on ordinary people, schools, organizations, universities, professors, and society. However, I think Confluent Education does leave a living legacy in the present in the following areas:

Institutionally it appears in identifiable and vigorous forms in several inspiring examples which I have identified. These few institutions are all free standing in the sense of autonomy from traditional academic institutions. And they all have become functionally autonomous from Confluent Education, although the links with Confluent Education are still discernible. All but one of the visionary founders/leaders had formal training in Confluent Education.

Professionally a new generation has taken the leadership of Confluent Education. However, I think it will be a struggle to achieve its expansionist goals in this time of so many similar movements and also backlashes to humanistically oriented programs. Although a solid professional legacy has been regenerated, there is a diminishing legacy in the local public schools and wide geographic dispersion of Confluently-trained people.

Culturally the Confluent legacy was most difficult to find and identify because of the diffusion of its effects with so many other similar influences (e.g., Gestalt institutes, Humanistic Psychology, Humanistic Education, Group Dynamics, NTL training, etc.).

I have discussed the very limited cultural legacy which I found in various archives and in considerable compatibility with certain approaches to history (see Appleby, p. 165). There is almost no detectable legacy to me in the sense of the arts (e.g., artifacts) or the humanities (e.g., history, literature, etc.) or in the broad sense of even Western popular cultures—At least I don't perceive any general cultural legacy which is distinguishable from whatever broad cultural effects the whole Human Potential Movement has had. In my studies, only a few archives remain specifically identifiable as having significant links with Confluent Education.

To me, there has been an impressive differentiation of institutional forms in the few that I studied. I see an original, common value base, firmly rooted in humanistic ideology and practice, and a strong current tendency toward spiritual/mystical forms (e.g., Pacifica, Concord Institute, the Meta-senter). I also see a definite international thrust from some of these institutions. Despite common ideological foundations, the diverse examples of the current "Confluent" institutions also suggest a significant functional autonomy from the original Confluent Education Program. They have all become "their own shops."

Visionary leadership, with all its assets and limitations, characterize the founders or current leaders of the institutions with a Confluent legacy. This is also true of the original visionary style of George I. Brown, founder and leader of the "parent" program in Confluent Education at UCSB.

In summary, to me, Confluent Education still has an identifiable and significant legacy, and in that legacy I find not only evidence that the particular institutions or professional groups can continue to flourish, but I regard these living legacies as a validation of Confluent Education—its mission, theories, and practices begun in the 1960s.

Chapter 5

Summary and Interpretation

Summary

This book relates the 27 year Confluent Education Program at UCSB to the broad Human Potential Movement, in which the program is considered to be deeply embedded. Both narrative and empirical perspectives are provided to document the program's essence and demise, and a cultural/contextual interpretation is offered as a framework for understanding these features and events.

The demise of the Confluent Education Program at UCSB was largely due to a clash of academic and professional subcultures, documented in Chapters 1 and 3. I see Confluent Education as a humanistic orientation, a relatively high-context learning community, but one surrounded by a hostile and/or indifferent low-context larger academic and community environment. When the influential senior professors retired, the program was promptly merged out of existence. This was a politically motivated move, supported by well-identified, conceptual and pragmatic—mostly long-term— weaknesses in the program, which, at best, had a difficult time surviving in a traditional academic subculture such as UCSB.

Most of the people drawn to this innovative, person-centered program were refugees from more traditional programs or professions. It was an "Intuitive-Feeling"-oriented subculture, perhaps a kind of counterculture in its earlier phases. Most of the students and Confluent faculty were highly satisfied with the experiential/affectively-based program, but much of the power structure in the academic establishment was critical, from the beginning.

Is there a viable model, "paradigm" for Confluent Education? I understand the concept of "paradigm" as a broadly representative, clear, classic, or exemplary underlying fundamental model. I see a paradigm as a kind of super-model, a "model of models" (i.e., a meta-model) as in "meta" analysis in Social Science Research. For example, consider the "Holocaust as a *paradigm* of evil." Or seeing physics as a *paradigmatic* physical science.

As I have pointed out in this book several times, from the very beginning of Confluent Education, people in it have been searching, and to this day continue to search, for an overarching model for this difficult-to-pin-down enterprise. I think the answer to this question depends on how this super-model (paradigm) is to be utilized. Is it primarily for an instructional guide as in De Muelle and Caston (1996) or is it mainly exploratory, as in A. Hillman, Weinstein's, and Yoemans' various models or my own "UNPACKING EXERCISE" (an ordinary language analysis)?

It seems to me that a paradigm for such a wide-ranging undertaking as Humanistic Education, Humanistic Psychology, or Confluent Education might be approached (broadly speaking) in two rather different ways. One could be the observational, intuitive subjective way in which most people in Confluent Education have approached this always intriguing but difficult task. And the other could be empirical/quantitative/measurement oriented with empirical claims.

In the latter category, there appear to be only two well-defined examples that I know of. These are my own OTL and other instrument-derived empirical models in this book (see pp. 8-10, 22-23) and the work of Phillip Moheno (1996), employing his HCIACS instrument (pp. 57-66).

Does this mean that since my and Moheno's paradigm for Confluent/Humanistic Education are the only ones empirically derived, they are the only ones (strictly speaking) that can make empirical claims via testable hypotheses? Are all the other models intuitively and subjectively derived incapable of being tested and heuristically validated? I think not!

Again, I think that validation of a paradigm depends on the purpose and intended use of that paradigm. In this sense, there is no (single) paradigm for Confluent Education and there might never be one. Much reflection and research must continue before we can clarify the whole issue of "paradigm"—and indeed, since there might well be different basic kinds of Confluent Education, our task will continue.

The origins of Confluent Education within the Human Potential Movement are traced from Aristotle to its current form. This is followed by what is intended to be a sustained and coherent critique of Confluent Education, including recent empirical surveys of attitudes toward it held by academics, students, and teachers in the field.

A detailed critique of the Confluent/humanistic approach revealed that experienced teachers in the field were highly critical of what they regarded as its impractical methods and jargon. Studies of other academics at UCSB and students in the program revealed that many were critical of the weak conceptual base and the impractical nature of much of the training. Most negative input was *not* directed at the people in the program, professors, students, etc. However, the negative critique was strong and, therefore, significant in my view.

As mentioned in Chapter 3, I felt that the most significant mistake we made was in separating ourselves from related research and scholarship and from other humanistic programs. When it came time for replacements, there were very few people capable of presenting Confluent Education in terms acceptable to the academy. We failed to establish and nurture a pool of qualified replacements. I see this as a symptom of our naïve elitism and defensive separatism.

The book concludes with the institutional, professional, and cultural legacy of Confluent Education and summarizes the "lessons to be learned" from the history of this innovative form of Humanistic Education.

The findings from studies of the legacy of Confluent Education revealed a strong and vibrant institutional legacy, epitomized in four "free standing" institutions. None were directly attached or even significantly connected with traditional research-based academia, which, in my view, accounts for their current survival and flourishing. There are relatively few such institutions, however, but they do indicate what potential such humanistic institutions have under favorable circumstances.

Professionally there is a living legacy in the new generation of professionals who have taken over and are struggling to regenerate Confluent Education. Also, in Chapter 4, I noted a hardy, but diminishing, band of humanistic/Confluent local teachers who carry the professional legacy of Confluent Education. Again, this supports the idea that there is a legacy but it is losing ground.

Whatever cultural legacy Confluent Education has is so amalgamated and diffused with other influences that it was very difficult for me to detect anything like an independent cultural legacy. Several impressive archives exist in this domain, but I see no separate evidence of a broad Confluent cultural legacy.

Apparently, a widely scattered group of Confluent institutions keep the legacy alive under the condition that they be self-started, autonomous from traditional academia and have visionary leaders, somewhat like George Brown, the founder of the "mother-program," Confluent Education.

The professional legacy is more problematic than the institutional legacy, and the cultural legacy is so hard to identify that it is almost negligible.

Lessons to be Learned

There are several major lessons to be learned from this historical perspective on Confluent Education. The first regards the name itself, which is metaphoric, vague, and refers to a pathological condition. This name has caused no end of confusion and difficulty for our program.

Closely following the ill-advised label for this approach is that the program did not fulfill its major mission: to integrate affect with cognition to improve teaching and learning. There was an affective bias in the program which depended too much for its identity on Gestalt Therapy as its most unique and prominent feature. The conceptual base was not well-formulated and, therefore, difficult to explain or defend. Insiders really *felt* what Confluent Education was and what it really could do, but communicating this to academics and professionals has remained problematic to this day.

On top of the identity problem and perhaps in reaction to this very problem, the program and people in it elevated it to a whole new genus, rather than another vital species of Humanistic Education with much to contribute as a *form* of Humanistic Education which, in turn, was an important component of the Human Potential Movement.

In this process, we elevated ourselves, cut ourselves off from our roots, and failed to draw strength from other similar programs. We, thereby, did not develop a substantial pool of qualified people to replace the three retiring senior professors.

Finally, from the perspective of this book, I now feel it would have been wiser to try to establish this historic program as a free-standing graduate program, or, once established, certainly not remaining within a traditional research-based institution like UCSB. I still think that UCSB is a dubious place for such an innovative, maverick program as Confluent Education.

The Place of Confluent Education in the Human Potential Movement

One major purpose of this book is to fill out, in detail, the historical, cultural, and philosophical context of Confluent Education, which included so many social science scholars, psychologists, educators, and philosophers generally overlooked in the UCSB program.

Another contribution lies in the completeness (background and texture) of the accounts of the origins, both remote and modern, and a sustained, coherent critique, neither of which can be found in other literature on Confluent Education and which I believe necessary for securing its identity.

Finally, the "clash of cultures" interpretation of the demise of the program in Confluent Education is supported by findings from empirical methodology. This includes multivariate analysis of the highly selective character of the students and survey research from students, professors, academic administrators, and classroom teachers. These studies document the perceived strength and weaknesses of the program, many of which characterized the Human Potential Movement per se. Also, this detailed critical agenda is missing in nearly all the Confluent literature.

The place of Confluent Education in the Human Potential Movement *is unique* in its specific form and function. There was *only one* complete academic program in Confluent Education and that was from 1966 to 1993.

It is *not unique* in the sense that other, similar programs in Humanistic Education flourished at the same time, which Strauss and Howe (1997, pp. 170-200) call the "Second Turning: Consciousness Revolution (1964-1984)." Strauss and Howe list six such "Awakenings," dating back to the 16th century, including the "Protestant Reformation," the "Transcendental Awakening," and the "Revolutionary Awakening." From the medieval past, similar "upheavals" were the Renaissance, and later the French and Scottish

Enlightenments and the Scientific Revolution in the Western World.

The Humanist Impulse

I refer to these awakenings or turnings as "The Humanist Impulse" in the history of our species.

The Humanist Impulse, like most overarching concepts, is subject to many interpretations and questions. For example, does the Industrial Revolution belong with the American and French Revolutions, the Renaissance, the Reformation, the French and Scottish Enlightenments, etc. as largely a manifestation of the Humanist Impulse in history?

I think that broad questions like this are both beyond my limited competence as a historian and the scope of this book. At the current stage of my development in 1998, I still see something I have termed the "Humanist Impulse" as a recurring, underlying, powerful urge of most cultures and societies whether it appeared in regular historical cycles like Strauss and Howe (1997) state or whether it arises in a cumulative, more or less linear fashion as seen by Fukuyama (1992).

As I have defined it in this book, the term "humanist" or "humanism" is very difficult to classify and delimit, so that it can be useful in a book like this. There are four essential definitions of humanism from which I have derived the idea of this recurring, irrepressible impulse. These definitions of humanism follow:

1. It begins with the *classical period in ancient Greece and Rome* which produced philosophers and scholars (Socrates, Plato, Aristotle, Herodotus, Thucydides, etc.) and continues through the Renaissance in the arts and various burgeoning forms of disciplines. So this is the classical/disciplinary definition.

2. A second definition refers to *political and religious liberties* also from the Renaissance, Reformation, French and American Revolutions, etc. Some of this was prompted by the growth of religious freedom—especially in Protestant Christianity.

3. The philosophy of *Secular (non-theistic) Humanism* is a related but distinguishable kind of Humanism with a tradition beginning after the Middle Ages and continuing into the present. It includes Scientific Revolutions (e.g., Copernicus, Darwin, Einstein, etc.).

4. Finally, there is the most recent (modern) form of *consciousness-revolutions*, which took place in the mid-1960s and lasted until the early 1980s. This is the kind of "touchy-feely" humanism which still

is part of the Human Potential Movement. It is this form which I think Confluent Education has always been deeply embedded.

But the Human Potential Movement itself, in its recent modern and post-modern forms, is in turn, a manifestation of the much broader Humanist Impulse which Lamont (1982) has referred to as the "Humanist Spirit" (pp. 19, 60).

So the Humanist Impulse has manifested itself in many and varied ways, such as a movement toward political liberty, Darwinian notions of evolutionary progress or New Age Psychology—including its spiritual, transpersonal manifestations.

Regardless of the form which the Humanist Impulse takes, I believe it is irrepressible and will occur even under the most discouraging conditions (e.g., ecological disaster, nuclear war, etc.). Confluent Education finally owes its energy, enterprise, and creativity to this grand impulse through its origins as a part of the Human Potential Movement. This then provides a historical context for The Place of Confluent Education in the Human Potential Movement.

So, my major conclusion is that Confluent Education is and was a part of its times, and very much part of something much larger, broader, and infinitely more significant in human history than this one of its many worthy offsprings.

References

Allport, G. W. (1937). *Personality: A psychological interpretation.* New York: Holt, Rinehart & Winston.

Allport, G. W. (1942). *The use of personal documents in psychological science.* New York: Social Science Research Council.

Allport, G. W. (1955). *Becoming: Basic considerations for a psychology of personality.* New Haven, CT: Yale University Press.

Allport, G. W. (1968). *The person in psychology; selected essays.* Boston: Beacon Press.

Alschuler, A. S. (Ed.). (1969). New directions in psychological education. *Educational Opportunities Forum.* Middletown, CT: Education Ventures.

Alschuler, A. S. (1970). *Teaching achievement motivation; theory and practice in psychological education.* Middletown, CT: Education Ventures.

Alschuler, A. S. (1973). *Developing achievement motivation in adolescents.* Englewood Cliffs, NJ: Educational Technology Publications.

Alschuler, A. S., Irons, R. B., McMullen, R., & Santiago-Wolpow, N. (1977). Collaborative problem solving as an aim of education in a democracy: The social literacy project. *Journal of Applied Behavioral Science, 13*(3), 315-326.

Anderson, W. T. (1983). *The upstart spring: Esalen and the American awakening.* Reading, MA: Addison-Wesley.

Appleby, J. D. (1997, Summer). The future of history. *Coastlines, 28*(1), 33.

Argyris, C. (1962). *Interpersonal competence and organizational effectiveness.* Homewood, IL: Irwin-Dorsey.

Argyris, C. (1964). *Integrating the individual and the organization.* New York: Wiley.

Argyris, C. (1971). *Management and organizational development.* New York: McGraw-Hill.

Argyris, C. (1976). *Increasing leadership effectiveness.* New York: Wiley.

Arnheim, R. (1974). "Gestalt" misapplied. *Contemporary Psychology, 19,* 570.

Back, K. (1972). *Beyond words: The story of sensitivity training and the encounter movement.* New York: Russell Sage Foundation.

Barott, J. E., & Kleiveland, J. (1996). The confluent approach to organizational change and development. In J. H. Brown, T. Yeomans, & L. Grizzard (Eds.), *Advances in confluent education: Integrating consciousness for human change* (pp. 63-80). Greenwich, CT: JAI Press.

Barrett, W. (1958). *Irrational man.* New York: Doubleday.

Bellah, R. N. et al. (1985). *Habits of the heart: Individualism and commitment in American life.* Berkeley, CA: University of California Press.

Bogad, S. R. (1975). Process in the classroom. In G. I. Brown, T. Yoemans, & L. Grizzard (Eds.), *The live classroom: Innovation through confluent education and gestalt* (p. 159). New York: Viking Press.

Borton, T. (1970). *Reach, touch, and teach: Student concerns and process education.* New York: McGraw-Hill.

Bradford, L., Gibb, J., & Benne, K. (Eds.). (1964). *T-group theory and laboratory method: Innovation in re-education.* New York: Wiley.

Brown, G. I. (Ed.). (1971). *Human teaching for human learning: An introduction to confluent education.* New York: Viking Press.

Brown, G. I. (Ed.). (1971). Introduction and Rationale. *Human teaching for human learning: An introduction to confluent education* (pp. 3-18). New York: Viking Press.

Brown, G. I. (1975). A cautionary conclusion. In G. I. Brown, T. Yoemans, & L. Grizzard (Eds.), *The live classroom: Innovation through confluent education and gestalt* (pp. 295-300). New York: Viking Press.

Brown, G. I. (1996). Foreword. In J. H. Brown (Ed.), *Advances in confluent education: Integrating consciousness for human change* (pp. ix-xiv). Greenwich, CT: JAI Press.

Brown, G. I., Phillips, M., & Shapiro, S. (1976). *Getting it all together: Confluent education.* Bloomington, IN: The Phi Delta Kappa Educational Foundation.

Brown, G. I., Yoemans, T., & Grizzard, L. (Eds.). (1975). *The live classroom: Innovation through confluent education and gestalt.* New York: Viking Press.

Brown, J. H. (1985). *External perceptions of the program in confluent education at U.C.S.B.* Unpublished masters project, University of California, Santa Barbara.

Brown, J. H. (Ed.). (1996). *Advances in confluent education: Integrating consciousness for human change.* Greenwich, CT: JAI Press.

Brown, J. R. (1996). *The I in science: Training to utilize subjectivity in research.* Oslo, Norway: Scandinavian University Press.

Bugental, J. F. T. (1963). Humanistic psychology: A new breakthrough. *American Psychologist, 18,* 563-567.

Bugental, J. F. T. (1964, Spring). The third force in psychology. *Journal of Humanistic Psychology, 4*(1), 19-26.

Bugental, J. F. T. (1965). *The search for authenticity.* New York: Holt, Rinehart &Winston.

Bugental, J. F. T. (1978). The third force in psychology. In I. D. Welch, G. Tate, & F. Richards (Eds.), *Humanistic psychology: A source book* (pp. 13-21). New York: Prometheus Books.

Bühler, C. (1959). Theoretical observations about life's basic tendencies. *American Journal of Psychotherapy, 13,* 561-581.

Bühler, C. (1965). Some observations on the psychology of the third force. *Journal of Humanistic Psychology, 5,* 54-56.

Bühler, C. (1967). Human life as a whole as a central subject of humanistic psychology. In. J. F. T. Bugental (Ed.), *Challenges of humanistic psychology* (pp. 83-92). New York: McGraw-Hill.

Bühler, C., & Allen, M. (1967). *Introduction to humanistic psychology.* New York: McGraw-Hill.

Child, I. L. (1973). *Humanistic psychology and the research tradition: Their several virtues.* New York: Wiley & Sons.

Chomsky, N. (1972). *Language and mind* (2nd ed.). New York: Harcourt, Brace, Jovanovich.

Coleman, A. M. (Ed.). (1994). *Companion encyclopedia of psychology, Vol. 2.* New York: Wiley & Sons.

Combs, A. W. (1962). A perceptual view of the adequate personality. In A. W. Combs (Ed.), *Perceiving, behaving, becoming* (pp. 50-64). Washington, DC: National Education Association.

Combs, A. W. (1971). New concepts of human potentials: New challenge for teachers. *Childhood Education, 47*(7), 349-355.

Combs, A. W. (1975). Humanistic goals of education. In D. A. Read & S. B. Simon (Eds.), *Humanistic education sourcebook* (pp. 91-100). Englewood Cliffs, NJ: Prentice Hall.

Combs, A. W. (1982). *A personal approach to teaching.* Boston: Allyn & Bacon.

Combs, A. W. (1988). Is there a future for humanistic or person-centered education? *Person-Centered Review, 3,* 96-103.

Combs, A. W. (1991). *The schools we need.* Lanham, MD: University Press of America.

Cox, H. (1973). Naked revival: Theology and the human potential movement. *The seduction of the spirit: The use and misuse of peoples religion.* New York: Simon & Schuster.

Darling, J. (1994). *Child-centered education and its critics.* London: Paul Chapman.

Darwin, C. (1956). *The origin of the species.* London: J. M. Dent. (Original work published 1859)

Davis, C. L. D. (1971). *Model for humanistic education. The Danish folk high school.* Columbus, OH: C. E. Merrill.

De Muelle, L., & Caston, M. D. (1996). Confluent education: A coherent vision of teacher education. In J. H. Brown (Ed.), *Advances in confluent education: Integrating consciousness for human change* (pp. 43-62). Greenwich, CT: JAI Press.

de Tocqueville, A. (1969). *Democracy in America* (G. Lawrence, Trans.). New York: Doubleday Books. (Original work published 1835, 1840).

Dewey, J. A. (1902). *The child and the curriculum.* Chicago: University of Chicago Press.

Dewey, J. A. (1922). *Human nature and conduct.* New York: Holt.

Dewey, J. A. (1926). *Democracy and education.* New York: Macmillan. (Original work published 1916)

Dewey, J. A. (1929). *Experience and nature.* New York: Norton.

Dewey, J. A. (1938). *Experience and education.* New York: Collier Books.

Dewey, J. A. (1956). *The school and society.* Chicago: University of Chicago Press. (Original work published 1900)

Dunne, J. S. (1973). *Time and myth.* New York: Doubleday.

Fairfield, R. P. (Ed.). (1971). *Humanistic frontiers in American education.* Englewood Cliffs, NJ: Prentice-Hall.

Frankel, C. (Ed.). (1947). *The social contract.* New York: Hafuer Press.

Frankl, V. E. (1963). *Man's search for meaning: An introduction to logo therapy* (I. Lasch, Trans.). New York: Washington Square Press.

Friedman, M. (1992). *Dialogue and the human image: Beyond humanistic psychology.* Newbury Park, CA: Sage.

Fukuyama, F. (1992). *The end of history and the last man.* New York: Free Press.

Gay, P. (Ed.). (1964). Some thoughts on education. *John Locke on education* (p. 39). New York: Columbia University, Teacher's College.

Goldstein, K. (1939). *The organism: A holistic approach to biology derived from pathological data in man.* New York: American Books.

Goldstein, K. (1940). *Human nature in the light of psychopathology.* Cambridge, MA: Harvard University Press.

Graham, H. (1986). *The human face of psychology in its historical, social and cultural contexts.* Philadelphia: Open University Press.

Groothuis, D. R. (1986). *Unmasking the new age: Is there a new religious movement trying to transform society?* Downers Grove, IL: Inter Varsity Press.

Gutek, G. L. (1968). How Gertrude teaches her children. *Pestalozzi and education* (p. 86). New York: Random House.

Hackbarth, S. (1996). Confluent education: An analysis from the perspective of Merleau—Ponty's philosophy. In J. H. Brown (Ed.), *Advances in confluent education: Integrating consciousness for human change* (pp. 18-19). Greenwich, CT: JAI Press.

Hall, E. T. (1959). *The silent language.* New York: Doubleday.

Hall, E. T. (1966). *The hidden dimension.* New York: Doubleday.

Hall, E. T. (1981). *Beyond culture.* New York: Doubleday.

Hall, E. T. (1983). *The dance of life.* New York: Doubleday.

Hart, T. (1996, Spring). The self as a research instrument [featured review article]. *The Humanistic Psychologist, 24*(1), 140-144.

Heidegger, M. (1962). *Being and time* (J. Macquarrie & E. Robinson, Trans.). New York: Harper & Row. (Original work published 1927)

Heidegger, M. (1977). Letter on humanism (F. Capuzzi & J. Gray, Trans.). In D. F. Krell (Ed.), *Martin Heidegger: Basic writings* (pp. 190-242). New York: Harper & Row. (Original work published 1947)

Henle, M. (1977). Gestalt psychology and gestalt therapy. *Journal of the History of the Behavioral Sciences, 14*, 23-32.

Hillman, A. W. (1973). *Confluent Education: A descriptive analysis of the concepts, goals and philosophy, and the relationship between them.* Unpublished doctoral dissertation, University of California, Santa Barbara, Education Department.

Hirsch, E. D., Jr. (1987). *Cultural literacy: What every American needs to know.* Boston: Houghton Mifflin.

Hirsch, E. D., Jr. (1996). *The schools we need: And why we don't have them.* New York: Doubleday.

Horney, K. (1937). *The neurotic personality of our time.* New York: W. W. Norton.

Horowitz, J., & Brown, J. H. (1996). Confluent education and evaluation research. In J. H. Brown (Ed.), *Advances in confluent education: Integrating consciousness for human change* (pp. 113-142). Greenwich, CT: JAI Press.

Husserl, E. (1962). *Phäuomenologische psychologie: Vorlesurgen sommersemester 1925.* Haag: Nijhoff.

Husserl, E. (1965). *Phenomenology and the crisis of philosophy* (Trans. with notes and an introduction by Quentin Lauer). New York: Harper Torchbooks.

Huxley, A. (1954). *The doors of perception.* New York: Harper & Brothers.

Iannaccone, L. (1996). A brief retrospection. In J. H. Brown (Ed.), *Advances in confluent education: Integrating consciousness for human change* (pp. 171-174). Greenwich, CT: JAI Press.

James, W. (1923). *The principles of psychology.* New York: Holt.

James, W. (1985). *The varieties of religious experience.* Cambridge, MA: Harvard University Press. (Original work published 1902)

Jarrett, J. L. (1973). *The humanities and humanistic education.* Reading, MA: Addison-Wesley.

Jaspers, K. (1954). *Way to wisdom: An introduction to philosophy* (R. Manheim, Trans.). New Haven, CT: Yale University Press.

Jaspers, K. (1957). Philosophical autobiography. In P. A. Schilpp (Ed.), *The philosophy of Karl Jaspers.* New York: Tudor.

Jones, R. M. (1968). *Fantasy and feeling in education.* New York: Harper & Row.

Joyce, B. R., Hersh, R. H., & McKibbin, M. (1983). *The structure of school improvement.* London: Longman.

Kang, S. J. (1992, April). *A crossed multilevel model for educational research.* Paper presented at the annual meeting of American Educational Research Association, San Francisco.

Kierkegaard, S. S. (1941). *Concluding unscientific postscript of the "philosophical fragments"* (D. F. Swenson, Trans.). Princeton, NJ: Princeton University Press.

Kierkegaard, S. S. (1944). *The concept of dread* (W. Lowrie, Trans.). Princeton, NJ: Princeton University Press.

Kiersy, D., & Bates, M. (1978). *Please understand me: Character and temperament types.* Del Mar, CA: Prometheus Nemesis Books.

Kilpatrick, W. H. (1918). The project method. *Teachers College Record, 19,* 318-334.

Kilpatrick, W. H. (1926). *Foundations of method.* New York: Macmillan.

Kilpatrick, W. H. (1930). "What do we mean by progressive education?" *Progressive Education, 7*(8), 383-386.

Kilpatrick, W. H. (Ed.). (1933). *The educational frontier.* New York: Appleton-Century-Crofts.

Koch, S. (1971). The image of man implicit in encounter group therapy. *Journal of Humanistic Psychology, 11*(2), 112-127.

Koffka, K. (1935). *Principles of gestalt psychology.* New York: Harcourt, Brace.

Kohlberg, L. (1971). Stages of moral development as a basis for moral education. In C. M. Beck (Ed.), *Moral education: Interdisciplinary approaches* (p. 44). Toronto: University of Toronto Press.

Köhler, W. (1929). *Gestalt psychology.* New York: Liveright.

Köhler, W. (1951). *The mentality of apes* (2nd rev. ed.) (E. Winter, Trans.). London: Routledge & Kegan Paul. (Original work published 1925)

Kolb, D. A. (1986). *Experiential learning: Experience as the source of learning and development.* Englewood Cliffs, NJ: Prentice-Hall.

Krathwohl, D. R., Bloom, B. S., & Masia, B. B. (1964). *Taxonomy of educational objectives. Handbook II: Affective domain.* New York: David McKay.

Kvernbekk, T. (1996). Confluent education: A participator view of knowledge. In J. H. Brown (Ed.), *Advances in confluent education: Integrating consciousness for human change* (pp. 1-15). Greenwich, CT: JAI Press.

Lamont, C. (1982). *The philosophy of humanism* (6th ed.). New York: Frederick Unger.

Lao Tsu. (1972). *Tao Teh Ching* (Gia-Fu-Feng & J. English, Trans.). New York: Random House.

Lasch, C. (1976, September). The narcissist society. *New York Review of Books*, 30.

Leonard, G. B. (1968). *Education and ecstasy.* New York: Delacorte Press.

Leonard, G. (1972). *The transformation.* New York: Delacorte Press.

Lewin, K. (1936). *Principles of topological psychology.* New York: McGraw-Hill.

Lewin, K. (1952). *Field theory in social science.* New York: McGraw-Hill.

Lieberman, M. A., Yalom, I. D., & Miles, M. B. (1973). *Encounter groups: First facts.* New York: Basic Books.

Loving, A. D., Sr. (1972). Foreword in J. R. Squire (Ed.), *A new look at progressive education*, ASCD 1972 Yearbook Committee. Washington, DC: Association for Supervision and Curriculum Development.

Lyon, H. C., Jr. (1971). *Learning to feel--feeling to learn.* Columbus, OH: Merrill.

Mann, J. H. (1979). Human potential. In R. J. Corsini (Ed.), *Current psychotherapies* (2nd ed.) (p. 521). Itasca, IL: F. E. Peacock.

Marin, P. (1975, October). The new narcissism. *Harpers*, 46.

Maslow, A. H. (1943). A theory of human motivation. *Psychological Review, 50*, 370-396.

Maslow, A. H. (1950). Self-actualizing people: A study of psychological health. *Personality Symposia* (Symposium #1 on Values). New York: Grune & Stratton.

Maslow, A. H. (1968). *Toward a psychology of being* (2nd ed.). New York: D. Van Nostrand.

Maslow, A. H. (1970). *Motivation and personality* (2nd ed.). New York: Harper & Row.

May, R. (Ed.). (1958). *Existence: A new dimension in psychiatry and psychology.* New York: Basics Books.

May, R. (1967). *Psychology and the human dilemma.* Princeton, NJ: Van Nostrand.

May, R. (1969a) *Existential psychology* (2nd ed.). New York: Random House.

May, R. (1969b). *Love and will.* New York: Norton.

May, R. (1972). *Power and innocence: A search for the sources of violence.* New York: Norton.

May, R. (1981). *Freedom and destiny.* New York: Norton.

McClelland, D. C. (1961). *The achieving society.* Princeton, NJ: Van Nostrand.

Merry, U., & Brown, G. I. (1987). *The neurotic behavior of organizations.* New York: Gardner Press.

Metz, G. (1975). Gestalt and the transformation. In G. I. Brown, T. Yoemans, & L. Grizzard (Eds.), *The live classroom: Innovation through confluent education and gestalt* (pp. 19-23). New York: Viking Press.

Miller, J. P. (1976). *Humanizing the classroom: Models of teaching in affective education.* New York: Praeger.

Mintz, A. (1973, July). Encounter groups and other panaceas. *Commentary,* 42.

Misiak, H., & Sexton, V. S. (1973). *Phenomenological, existential and humanistic psychologies: A historical survey.* New York: Gruue & Stratton.

Moheno, P. B. B. (1985). *An exploratory study into the correspondence between humanistic teaching values and humanistic teaching behaviors in secondary math and science teachers.* Unpublished doctoral dissertation, University of California, Santa Barbara.

Moheno, P. B. B. (1996). *Educating our 21st century adventurers.* Lanham, MD: University Press of America.

Moreno, J. L. (1946). *Psychodrama.* New York: Beacon House.

Mosher, R. L., & Sprinthall, N. A. (1971). Psychological education: A means to promote personal development during adolescence. *The Counseling Psychologist, 2*(4), 3-82.

Murphy, G. (1949). *Historical introduction to modern psychology.* New York: Harcourt, Brace & World.

Murray, H. A. et al. (1938). *Explorations in personality: A clinical and experimental study of fifty men of college age.* New York: Oxford University Press.

Neill, A. S. (1960). *Summerhill: A radical approach to child rearing.* New York: Hart.

Nevill, D. D. (Ed.). (1977). *Humanistic psychology: New frontiers.* New York: Gardner Press.

Newberg, N. (1977). *Affective education in Philadelphia.* Bloomington, IN: The Phi Delta Educational Foundation.

Nietzsche, F. W. (1896). *Thus spake zarathustra, A book for all and none.* New York: Macmillan.

Noll, J. W., & Kelly, S. P. (Eds.). (1970a). The education of a Christian prince. *Foundations of education in America.* New York: Harper & Row.

Noll, J. W., & Kelly, S. P. (Eds.). (1970b). The great didactic. *Foundations of education in America.* New York: Harper & Row.

Nuttin, J. (1962). *Psychoanalysis and personality: A dynamic theory of normal personality* (Rev. ed., G. Lamb, Trans). New York: Sheed & Ward.

Otto, H. A. (1970). *Group methods to actualize human potential.* Beverly Hills, CA: Herbert A. Otto.

Patterson, C. H. (1973). *Humanistic education.* Englewood Cliffs, NJ: Prentice Hall.

Perls, F. S. (1947). *Ego, hunger and aggression.* New York: Random House.

Perls, F. S. (1969). *Gestalt therapy verbatim.* Lafayette, CA: Real People Press.

Perls, F. S. (1973). *The gestalt approach and eye witness to therapy.* Palo Alto, CA: Science & Behavior Books.

Perry, J. W. (1976). *Roots of renewal in myth and madness.* San Francisco: Jossey-Bass.

Piaget, J. (1967). The significance of John Amos Comenius at the present time. In introduction to *John Amos Comenius on education* (p. 10). New York: Bureau of Publications, Teacher's College, Columbia University.

Plowden Report: Central Advisory Council for Education (England). (1967). *Children and their primary schools.* London: Her Majesty's Stationery Office. (Generally referred to as the Plowden Report after Lady Bridget Plowden)

Plumb, L. D. (1993). *A critique of the human potential movement.* New York: Garland Publishing, Inc.

Popenoe, J. (1970). *Inside Summerhill.* New York: Hart.

Popplestone, J. A., & McPherson, M. W. (1988). *Dictionary of concepts in general psychology.* New York: Greenwood.

Raths, L. E., Harmin, M., & Simon, S. G. (1966). *Values and teaching.* Columbus, OH: Merrill.

Raudenbush, S. W. (1988). Educational applications of hierarchical linear models: A review. *Journal of Educational Statistics, 13*(2), 85-116.

Reaching New Heights. (1997, September 23). *Santa Barbara News-Press.*

Read, D. A., & Simon, S. B. (1975). *Humanistic education sourcebook.* Englewood Cliffs, NJ: Prentice Hall.

Reich, W. (1949). *Character analysis.* New York: Noonday Press.

Roberts, T. B. (Ed.). (1975). *Four psychologies applied to education.* New York: Schenkman.

Rogers, C. R. (1961). *On becoming a person.* Boston: Houghton Mifflin.

Rogers, C. R. (1969). *Freedom to learn.* Columbus, OH: Charles R. Merrill.

Rogers, C. R. (1983). *Freedom to learn for the 80's.* Columbus, OH: Merrill.

Rogers, C. R. (1985). Toward a more human science of the person. *Journal of Humanistic Psychology, 15,* 7-24.

Rosen, R. (1997, July 28). Chipping away at historical amnesia. *The Los Angeles Times,* p. 80.

Royce, J. R., & Mos, L. P. (1981). *Humanistic psychology: Concepts and criticisms.* New York: Plenum Press.

Samples, R. E. (1970, September). Tools for everyone [Review of the book *Reach, Touch and Teach*]. *Saturday Review,* 82.

Sartre, J-P. (1943). *Being and nothingness.* New York: Philosophical Library.

Sartre, J-P. (1947). *No exit* (S. Gilbert, Trans.). New York: Alfred A. Knopf.

Sartre, J-P. (1953). *Existential psychoanalysis.* New York: Philosophical Library.

Schutz, W. C. (1967). *Joy.* New York: Grove Press.

Shapiro, S. B. (1975). Developing models by unpacking confluent education. In G. I. Brown, T. Yoemans, & L. Grizzard (Eds.), *The live classroom: Innovation through confluent education and gestalt* (pp. 109-120). New York: Viking Press.

Shapiro, S. B. (1984). *The training effects (on the OTL) of one academic year on the instructional values of MA and credential students in education.* Unpublished manuscript, University of California, Santa Barbara.

Shapiro, S. B. (1985a, Winter). An empirical analysis of operating values in humanistic education. *Journal of Humanistic Psychology, 25*(1), 94-108.

Shapiro, S. B. (1985b, Winter). The development and validation of an instrument to measure student orientation to humanistic instructional values. *Educational and Psychological Measurement, 45*(4), 869-880.

Shapiro, S. B. (1985c). *A factor-analytic comparison of experts and students on fifteen humanistic instructional values.* Unpublished manuscript, University of California, Santa Barbara.

Shapiro, S. B. (1986, June). Survey of basic instructional values in humanistic education. *Journal of Humanistic Education and Development, 24*(4), 144-158.

Shapiro, S. B. (1987). The instructional values of humanistic educators: An expanded empirical analysis. *Journal of Humanistic Education and Development, 25*(3), 155-170.

Shapiro, S. B. (1997). The UCSB confluent education program: Its essence and demise. *The Journal of Humanistic Psychology, 37*(3), 79-104.

Shapiro, S. B., & Fitzgerald, L. F. (1989, Summer). The development of an objective scale to measure a transpersonal orientation to learning. *Educational and Psychological Measurement, 49*(2), 375-384.

Shapiro, S. B., & Mortola, P. J. (1996). The place of group dynamics in confluent education. In J. H. Brown (Ed.), *Advances in confluent education: Integrating consciousness for human change* (pp. 81-94). Greenwich, CT: JAI Press.

Shiflett, J. M., & Brown, G. I. (1972). *Confluent education: Attitudinal and behavioral consequences of confluent teacher training.* University Center, MI: University Center Monograph Series, Saginaw Valley State College.

Shur, E. (1976). *The awareness trap: Self-absorption instead of social change.* New York: Quadrangle.

Siepmann, K. B. (Ed.). (1987). *Benét's Reader's Encyclopedia* (3rd. ed.) (pp. 735-756). New York: Harper & Row.

Silberman, C. E. (1970). *Crisis in the classroom.* New York: Random House.

Simon, S., Howe, L., & Kirschenbaum, H. (1972). *Values clarification: A handbook of practical strategies.* New York: Hart.

Simpson, E. L. (1976). *Humanistic education: An interpretation.* Cambridge, MA: Ballinger Publishing Co.

Skinner, B. F. (1948). *Walden two.* New York: Macmillan.

Smith, E. W. L. (Ed.). (1976). *The growing edge of gestalt therapy.* New York: Brunner/Mazel.

Smith, M. B. (1991). *Values, self and society: Toward a humanist social psychology.* New Brunswick, NJ: Transaction Publishers.

Squire, J. R. (Ed.). (1972). *A new look at progressive education.* ASCD 1972 Yearbook Committee. Washington, DC: Association for Supervision and Curriculum Development.

Strauss, W., & Howe, N. (1997). *The fourth turning.* New York: Broadway Books.

Sutich, A. (1962). American Association for Humanistic Psychology: Articles of Association. *Journal of Humanistic Psychology, 2,* 96-97.

Sutich, A., & Vich, M. (Eds.). (1969). *Readings in humanistic psychology.* New York: Free Press.

Suzuki, D. (1965). *The training of the Zen Buddhist monk.* New York: University Books.

Tageson, C. W. (1982). *Humanistic psychology: A synthesis.* Homewood, IL: Dorsey press.

Tannenbaum, R., & Schmidt, W. (1958, March-April). How to choose a leadership pattern. *Harvard Business Review, 36,* 95-101.

Tannenbaum, R., Weschler, I., & Massarik, F. (1961). *Leadership and organization.* New York: McGraw-Hill.

Weinstein, G., & Fantini, M. D. (1968). *The disadvantage: Challenge to education.* New York: Harper & Row.

Weinstein, G., & Fantini, M. D. (Eds.). (1970). *Toward humanistic education: A curriculum of affect.* New York: Praeger.

Wertheimer, M. (1965). Experimental studies on seeing of motion (D. Cantor, Trans.). In R. J. Herrustein & E. G. Boring (Eds.), *A source book in the history of psychology* (pp. 163-168). Cambridge, MA: Harvard University Press. (Original work published 1912)

Wertz, F. J. (Guest Editor). (1992, Summer/Autumn). The humanistic movement in psychology. *The Humanistic Psychologist* 20(2 & 3), 474.

Winkler, F. E. (1960). *Man: The bridge between two worlds.* New York: Harper & Brothers.

Yoemans, T. R. (1973). *Toward a confluent theory of the teaching of English.* Unpublished doctoral dissertation, University of California, Santa Barbara, Education Department.

Yoemans, T. R. (1975a). Search for a working model: Gestalt, psychosynthesis, and confluent education. In G. I. Brown, T. Yoemans, & L. Grizzard (Eds.), *The live classroom: Innovation through confluent education and gestalt* (pp. 132-158). New York: Viking Press.

Yoemans, T. R. (1975b). Gestalt theory and practice and the teaching of literature. In G. I. Brown, T. Yoemans, & L. Grizzard (Eds.). *The live classroom: Innovation through confluent education and gestalt* (pp. 80-90). New York: Viking Press.

Name Index

Subject Index

Biographical Sketch of the Author

Stewart B. Shapiro, Ph.D. grew up in a small city in Pennsylvania, completed his B.S. degree at the local college and his M.S. degree in Psychology at Pennsylvania State University. He was a psychologist in the U.S. Army for 3 1/2 years during WWII. Dr. Shapiro received his Ph.D. in Clinical Psychology in 1950 at the University of Southern California, and practiced for 17 years as a Humanistic Clinical Psychologist in the Los Angeles area. In 1967, he became a professor at the University of California, Santa Barbara and joined the program in Confluent (Humanistic) Education, where he served until his retirement in 1991.

Dr. Shapiro has also practiced as an organizational consultant since 1965 and led many personal growth seminars at Esalen and other similar facilities.

From the beginning of his academic career, Dr. Shapiro has been investigating the underlying values of Confluent Education, culminating in the current book. He has published many articles and a few books on models of Humanistic and Confluent Education. His most recent article was on the Essence and Demise of the Confluent Education Program at UCSB, published in *The Journal of Humanistic Psychology*. This book is an expansion of that article.